# Flower Arranging

## OTHER CONCORDE GARDENING BOOKS

# Flower Arranging

## Michael Goulding

WARD LOCK LIMITED·LONDON

© Ward Lock Limited 1978

First published in Great Britain in 1978
by Ward Lock Limited, 116 Baker Street,
London W1M 2BB, a member of the Pentos
Group.

House editor Teresa Mozley
Text filmset in Times New Roman/Times Bold
by Computer Photoset Limited, Birmingham

Printed and bound in Hong Kong
by Mandarin Publishers Ltd.

**British Library Cataloguing in Publication Data**

Goulding, Michael
    Flower arranging–(Concorde books)
    1. Flower arrangement
  I. Title  II. Series
  745.92      SB449

   ISBN  0–7063–5546–6 Pbk
         0–7063–5544–X

# Contents

# 1 Equipment

## SCISSORS, SECATEURS

Nothing saddens me more than when I see shrubs, trees and flowers broken or torn off at the stem. Not only does it leave the bush or tree with an ugly tear, but it will be followed by a certain amount of die-back. This is a sight which seems to occur annually in the pussy willow (salix) massacre. Directly the trees start to produce their silky buds, it is the sign for the 'break off, let's take some home' brigade to move in on our woods and hedgerows. If only everyone would have good small pruning shears or secateurs with them, then a neat cut would avoid a lot of damage. Whenever you go into your own garden or the countryside to pick foliage and flowers, go equipped–which leads me to the mechanics of arranging.

Firstly, equipment, beginning with those secateurs, scissors or pruning shears. There is a wide selection of these implements on the market, so as long as they are sharp and easily carried in your pocket, choose the model you like. One of the main essentials of a cutting implement is that it should not only cut flowers, but also wire netting and wire because, more often than not, after you have picked your flowers you will be searching for a piece of wire netting to fill a vase. When you have the urge to arrange a vase of flowers, you need to be able to choose one quickly before the inspiration you had whilst picking the flowers in the garden has vanished; it is therefore much more satisfactory to find the vase of your choice ready wired and clean waiting to be used. Then again it works the other way round. Sometimes when you survey your vases, and your eye happens to fall on, perhaps, a white china basket, you think how pretty it would be arranged with a posy of grey foliage and pale mauve clematis, and off you rush to the garden to see if you can carry out the idea. So choose the cutting implement with which you are happiest, and keep it well sharpened.

Try to remember to have your scissors or small pruning shears with you, especially if you are going out to do a vase or, maybe, to a place where you are unable to obtain them in a hurry. On two occasions this has happened to me, and it has taught me a lesson; so now its scissors and secateurs first, flowers second. The first occasion was at the Paris Floralies where I was exhibiting a vase of flowers. Not only had my flowers and vase been despatched back to England by mistake, but later on, when I had at last retrieved them and I came to cut my wire netting for the vase, I found to my horror I had no scissors and that time was against me, so I had to undo and twist the wire by hand! The other time that I forgot my scissors was on my first job as a professional flower arranger, and I had to break every stem of foliage and flowers with my teeth!

## CHOOSING OF FLOWER SUPPORTS AND CONTAINERS

The choice of a suitable container will make or mar your arrangement. Let me give you an instance. When I was learning the art of arranging flowers at the Constance Spry School – happily at the time when Mrs Spry herself was still alive – I, together with the others in my class, was given a collection of marguerites and grasses to arrange. We were told to choose our own vases, so off we rushed to the cupboard and all chose what we thought was a suitable container. I, obviously with a grand outlook, chose a vase which, in retrospect, would have been more suitable in a church with an arrangement of lilies for a wedding than my bunch of daisies. Much to our chagrin, one by one our choice of vases was criticised and frowned upon until, exasperated, our instructor said: 'I can do no more except to tell you that you have all failed miserably in your choice,' and her parting shot was: 'Hasn't anybody heard of a basket?' There, standing all alone on a shelf shunned by us all, was a delightful wicker basket crying

8

out to be arranged with the daisies and grasses. I learnt a great deal from this lesson, and I hope it will stand you in good stead as you reach for a vase to match your flowers and your room.

## PEDESTALS

Pedestals play a very important part in various aspects of flower decoration because such a piece of equipment will enable you to raise up an arrangement so that it can be seen by everyone, especially when you know that a room, hall or a church is going to be full of people. A good point here is that when you are standing in a room thinking where the flowers should be placed, just stand for a moment and think of the room full of people, then see where you can place them to be seen to advantage by all. So often in my professional career it has been suggested to me 'wouldn't the fireplace be a good place to put them?' I try to point out that the mantle shelf would be better, and explain that there the flowers will be above the guests instead of below them.

## OASIS

This is a splendid form of trapped water which can be used to effect where you need an arrangement of flowers when perhaps a vase cannot be used – marvellous for a wall arrangement or a shallow shelf too small for a vase. It is also an asset when you have a small vase which does not hold enough water. I personally think it should be used only where a vase containing wire is not possible. This reminds me of the time when I was asked to provide a background of foliage and flowers for a film depicting diamonds. I was shown a magnificent brooch made by the famous Russian court jeweller Fabergé of a spray of snowdrops; the flowers themselves were of pearls, the stem and leaves of diamonds. The inspiring aspect about it was that all the flowers were on springs and had a shimmering movement; to me, the most important facet of arranging flowers is that they should move. Oasis does not help in this way, but in many instances it is a godsend.

First you must give the oasis a good soak, then let it drain. If using a vase, place your wire netting in first so that you have a layer at the base; then place the block of oasis on top, crush the wire netting on top of that and tie it in. If using it without a vase, wrap the whole block with 2·5 cm/1 in wire netting just like a parcel, and stand it in a shallow tin. If the oasis is going against a surface that will mark, cover the back with polythene. Dry oasis can be restored by soaking it in hot water.

## WIRE NETTING

I think that this is the easiest and most satisfactory of all aids to holding flowers in vases. A large mesh 4 cm/1½ in is usually best; it should be firm enough to crumple up to place in a vase and, at the same time, firm enough to hold your flowers and foliage. It is obtainable from most hardware shops. Together with a roll of silver gauge 32, and a roll of plastic coated wire, with a container – no matter what it is, from a Grecian marble tazza through to a jam jar! – if you have good wire netting fixed in really firmly you are more than halfway to a successful arrangement. When placing wire netting in a vase, get it in a cone-shape first, then place the end of the wire on the base of the vase. Carry on pushing the wire in until you have a series of layers, ending up with the other end tucked in and raised above the rim of the vase, leaving the final top dome-shaped. This will enable the flowers to have the maximum support and therefore they will not move when being arranged. When you have made this layered structure, tie it in with whichever gauge wire suits the vase. A good test is that you should be able to pick up your vase, whether it be lead or crystal, by its wire netting.

This reminds me of an unfortunate experience I had when I was pushing wire netting down into a rather beautiful tazza-shaped vase made of pink marble. The owner was watching me to see how it was done; I pushed the wire netting into the bowl part, and I must have pressed too hard because the whole vase disintegrated under the weight! So please remember the gentle touch where you have a delicate or valuable vase – and maybe have a good insurance policy!

At the time of writing this book I was asked to participate in a Flower Festival at my local Abbey of St Alban's. While I was arranging my vase I was interrupted more than once to give advice to some of the other arrangers, and the question

A late summer posy of mixed cream and apricot flowers and foliage arranged in a small bronze *tazza* on a marble base. The flowers are rose 'Peace', dimorphotheca, dahlia, border pinks, *Polygonum affine* and chincherinchee. Foliage are *Lonicera* 'Aureo-reticulata', variegated ivies, *Begonia rex* leaf, erica, *Senecio greyii*, ballota, with some early sprays of *Viburnum farreri* and late flowers of abelia. This small posy is the greatest joy to arrange as it takes in late, and early flowers, mixed house plant foliage and garden shrubs, together with shop-bought dimorphothecas, chincherinchees and border pinks. When they are mixed with home-grown foliage and flowers, as shown in the illustration, they marry into one.

11

I was most frequently asked was: 'Why is it that my tube on a stick is wobbling about?' This was, so I found, because instead of placing the wire netting in the vase first, then adding the oasis, they had just covered the oasis with the wire. It is essential to give support to the stick at the bottom as well as the top of the vase, so put your wire netting in first. If you do it the other way, though it may seem firm when first stuck into the oasis, it will become wobbly as the oasis will crack as you poke your flowers and foliage into it. Start your outline well towards the back of the vase in order to get it sitting well and not leaning forward. This is very important as time and time again I have seen vases leaning forward because the vase and oasis were inadequate for the quantity of material to be used.

## HANGING BASKETS

These are a joy, especially in the summer time, in a marquee for a wedding or a hall for a dance if there is a suitable place to hang them. They are above the guests' heads, create a gala feeling, and also have the ability to lower a ceiling. Choose an ordinary wire one, similar to the ones used in the garden for hanging plants, fill the base with a little sphagnum moss, and rest two blocks of well-soaked oasis side by side with a piece of 2·5cm/1in mesh wire netting at the top. Arrange your flowers in a ball-shape, remembering to place the flowers looking downwards; fill in with pale green ferns or light foliage. For the supports use galvanised wire and hang it with a paper waterproof ribbon usually available from most good florists.

## VASES

There has been a tremendous amount written in the past about vases and various needs for helping the arranger. In my opinion the most important aspect of any container is depth so that your flowers can get enough water. Anything goes so far as vases are concerned, but wide-topped ones enable you to obtain a flowing effect; they also give more space, and more scope for a natural arrangement. On the other hand they do need more flowers, so that leads us on to consider smaller containers.

12

## SILVER, BRASS AND COPPER

Silver has great depth, and many delightful shapes and sizes can be found; a silver Victorian basket filled with catkins and Christmas roses is heaven-sent for a dining-table. Old soup tureens, or delicate tracery baskets lined with Bristol blue glass, can be a marvellous foil for violets and grape hyacinths. The texture of brass and copper, on the other hand, is an appealing contrast for different grasses, seed pods, and dried flowers of rich autumn colours. At the other end of the year, a copper bowl filled with daffodils, catkins and berried ivy is a herald of spring.

## GLASS

The only drawback to glass is that it is essential to keep the water clear if the vase is to be seen; but glass bowls filled with garden pinks or sweet peas are lovely. A specimen vase is ideal for displaying a single flower or stem of *Chimonanthus praecox* (wintersweet), or a stem of *Garrya elliptica* whose catkins so enchanted Wedgwood that he used them many times as a decoration on his china ware as a garland. When using a tall glass container, try and fix the wire netting at the top of the vase so that the stems can be seen in a criss-cross fashion, adding another dimension to your arrangement. A few drops of household bleach will help to keep the water clear for a time.

Writing about glass vases reminds me of a time when I was arranging flowers for a lady who was giving a dance. I noticed that she had in her drawing-room two 120 cm/4 ft tall glass vases with just two or three branches of stripped lime. The dark brown stems under the water reflected in the glass, and the pale lime green flowers and branches looked quite magnificent in their simplicity.

## BASKETS

Baskets are wonderful for holding simple wild and garden flowers, or in the autumn, fruits and flowers with their leaves and possibly one or two *Cobaea scandens* flowers. Polyanthus dug up in bloom can be planted in baskets; but remember to line them with polythene, or have a zinc lining made for your favourite basket.

## CHINA

Today, in many junk shops and, of course, depending on the size of your purse, antique shops, beautiful bowls, tureens, vegetable dishes, and white china vases in all shapes can be found and become treasured possessions of the vase cupboard. The Victorians were great makers of many pieces of ornamental china which we now use as vases. I have a beautiful white china vase in the shape of two shells held up by coral which looks so lovely filled with a mixture of pale green leaves and cream flowers, or a few stems of pink Japanese azaleas with deep purple *Begonia* leaves.

## METAL TUBES

These are an absolute joy to help extend the length of your flowers or foliage especially when arranging a large group of flowers in a vase. They can be used just as they are, poked into the wire netting, or attached to square-sided sticks by wire or tape to stop them swinging around; then the tube attached to the stick is threaded through the wire netting to give it a good support. Several of these can be used in one vase, and also be supported by single tubes to give added strength to the tubes on sticks.

## PINHOLDERS

These are a useful type of flower holder. They have a solid base covered with sharp spikes and are most suitable for putting in shallow bowls and dishes. To stop the pinholder from moving around, oasis fix can be used to secure it in the bowl or dish. The pinholders come into their own when using two or three stems of flowers such as wisteria or tulips; but you will need to find a leaf or a piece of driftwood to hide the pinholder.

This arrangement of mixed white and green flowers with silver foliage was one of a pair that I had been asked to do in Westminster Cathedral for the Jubilee Flower Festival where I was representing the United Kingdom. At the same time I was sponsored by the Royal Horticultural Society, which meant that, fortunately, I had the Society's garden at Wisley to pick from. The main framework was made of magnificent stems of *Cornus kousa* and *Philadelphus coronarius*, with *Senecio greyii*. There were stems of angelica seed heads, spears of *Phormium tenax*, white delphinium, white foxgloves, auratum lilies, arum lilies, white paeonias and spathiphyllum flowers. For silver leaves a plant of *Caladium* 'Candidum', surrounded by a white hydrangea plant, and a white lace-cap hydrangea. The arrangements were done in two cast-iron bird baths on 1·5 m/5 ft oak pedestals. The flowers were held by a framework of metal tubes strapped on to wooden sticks and held firmly in place by a structure of 5 cm/2 in mesh wire netting. In the right-hand corner of the picture you can just see a piece of a 1·8 m/6 ft cross we made entirely of white stock stems. The base of the cross was of oasis bricks covered by 2·5 m/1 in mesh wire netting.

# 2 Practical Points, Conditioning of Flowers, Colouring and Texture

## CUTTING AND SMASHING STEMS

Always cut your stems on the slant so that they get maximum water intake when in the vase. Where woody stems are concerned cutting is not sufficient, so it is necessary to use a hammer or wooden mallet and gently crush the stems of flowering shrubs, evergreens, chrysanthemums, stocks, roses and paeonies – in fact, any types with hard stems.

If cutting your flowers from the garden for arrangements, try and cut them the day before you need them so as to give them time for a good drink. There are two opinions about when to cut them – early morning or early evening. I prefer the early evening as the flower has been able to build up a good supply of food through the day, especially if the sun has been shining. Furthermore, one has more time to pick in the evening and, of course, the flowers have all night to have a drink. If you prefer the early morning, cut before the dew has dried on the flower and before the sun is up.

A word here about the idea of cutting the stems of certain flowers under water. Sweet peas love this treatment, so do anthuriums. It stops the formation of air bubbles which collect in the stem when cutting above water. These bubbles can prevent the flow of water up the stems, causing withering. (See also the notes under Practical Points.) Remove any excess foliage that will be submerged in the water.

## MIST SPRAYERS

These are very useful, especially in hot weather, to keep a cool, moist air around an arrangement and prevent undue loss of moisture through the flowers and foliage; they also increase

16

humidity. If you are trying to force early flowering shrubs such as forsythia, cherry or guelder rose, spraying them will help to keep the wood and buds moist, thus enabling them to bloom early without the wood drying out. Humidity plays a very important part in prolonging the life of flowers.

## SHORTENING FLOWERS

I think that it is a great mistake to be too ready to cut your material. To avoid this, try threading the flowers through your wire netting support, placing them deeper in the vase at an angle so that they flow out of your arrangement, giving a gentler and more flowing line. At the same time this enables the flowers, branches or foliage to take up more water. Graduate your flowers in the vase so that each one is seen to the full, with plenty of 'in and out' flowers so that the overall look of the arrangement creates space and movement.

Remember you can always shorten a stem, but you cannot lengthen it! When next you do a vase, try doing it without cutting any one of the flowers, then you will get the idea.

## ARRANGING FLOWERS: LINE, PROPORTION

I have always found the easiest way to get your outline is to place in position two or three flowers first – say, two in the centre and one either side to get a general shape. Then you can fill in from there, always keeping your centre free until the last. This has three good points: 1) your centre is the focal point to place your special last flowers so that they do not get lost; 2) as you keep putting your hand in to place the next flower or piece of foliage, you do not keep brushing past your centre flowers and therefore you avoid bruising them; 3) you have space until the end, to see where you are going. For a bowl or oval dish keep your centre low.

The four chief principles of arranging flowers are Design, Scale, Balance and Harmony.

**Design** is the shape it must look – not as though it's just happened, but to give the feeling that the flowers and foliage have been planned.

**Scale** is the selection of the materials; flowers, foliage, vase,

Summer galaxy of apricot, coral and white flowers with pale green foliages. This antique plant holder, standing in the drawing-room of a lovely Queen Anne shooting box, was arranged by me in early July. It consisted of a framework of stripped lime, which when stripped of its own leaves, left fragrant yellowish-white clusters of flowers. Branches of *Philadelphus coronarius*, stems of moluccella, bells of Ireland, two stems of *Rodgersia pinnata* 'Superba' seed heads, together with angelica seed pods. Also in with the foliage are stems of Solomon's seal, polygonatum, hosta leaves, *Hosta sieboldiana*. The flowers were *Lilium auratum* and *L. regale*, white delphiniums, eremurus, the coral 'Highdown Hybrids', coral pink gerberas, flame *Lilium* 'Enchantment', and stems of montbretia flowers, *Crocosmia masonorum*, and in the centre is a plant of a croton, *Codiaeum pictum*. A framework of $3 \cdot 8 \, \text{cm}/1\frac{1}{2}$ in mesh wire netting was used in the metal container which held the water. I used warm water with some sugar to help the lasting quality of the delphiniums. The height of the group was about $1 \cdot 8 \, \text{m}/6 \, \text{ft}$ without the container.

18

Midsummer glory at Blenheim Palace designed as one of a pair for a ball. The foundation was constructed of four square frames of wood with 3·8 cm/ 1½ in mesh wire netting stretched across to hold three blocks of oasis. These were placed at regular intervals down a square pole which stood 2 m/7 ft high, and this was then positioned firmly in a white 'Versailles' type tub. The overall height when dressed with flowers was in the region of 6 m/20 ft. The colouring was white, pink and blue, and the flowers used were *Lilium regale*, white delphiniums *Paeonia* 'Sarah Bernhardt', *Delphinium* 'Blue Bee', pink carnations and Gypsophila. The foliage was of *Escallonia* 'Apple Blossom', with pots of *Hydrangea* 'White Lace Cap', pink *Hydrangea hortensia* and pink caladiums. To create the required shape we started by using the white delphiniums to get the height, *Lilium regale* to form the width and shape, the plants to give shape, form and depth; the rest of the flowers and foliage added more form and colour. These pyramids of flowers lasted several days, needing just a fine spray of water each day. I used these stands as I thought that the effect would be bolder in concept than the usual vase standing on a pedestal—which incidentally, on reflection, would have looked out of place in these surroundings.

19

that are in proportion to each other ie you would not put gladioli with freesias.

**Balance:** whether it is an all-over design or a one-sided one, they should both balance. Balance speaks for itself. Your creation, however lovely, must look comfortable and 'sit' well; in fact, be well-balanced.

**Harmony:** colour is the key note here. A good eye is needed to choose a combination of colours which is pleasing, also the ability to choose suitable flowers, ie those of the same season. What more suitable a match in the spring than forsythia and tulips? So much better than forsythia and carnations. Carnations are lovely in the summer either on their own or in a glorious summer mixture, just as chrysanthemums are right in the autumn.

To sum up, get your flowers in proportion to your vase. A height of approximately one and a half times is a good guide. In general, make your vase part of the arrangement; nothing is worse than when you can see your flowers leaving the vase. Never have the flowers too wide or too high for your vase, or out of proportion with the vase or background, or you will ruin your desired effect.

## CHOOSING FLOWERS

When you go into your florist's shop to choose your flowers, and most shops sell flowers by the stem and not by the bunch, have a plan in your head of what flowers and foliage you require, and also the colour. A good tip when doing a mixed arrangement is to choose as many shapes as possible, then your flowers will complement each other. Let us suppose you are doing an apricot and cream arrangement in early summer for a large vase suitable for a piano, you would need, say, three stems guelder rose, two stems whitebeam (sorbus) two trails of ivy, two stems Solomon's seal, five stems silver foliage, (*Senecio greyii*) five artichoke leaves, two regale lilies, three stems of stocks, three trails of roses and three paeonies, which give you all your shapes – round, trumpet, straight, and trailing foliage.

When you have finished your arrangement, stand back and

study it to see whether you have hidden your wire netting, that you have not left any gaps, and that there are not any broken leaves or a flower left dangling. Finally, remember to fill the vase with water. It is advisable to fill your vase only two-thirds full before starting your arrangement as the level of the water will rise from the many stems.

## PLACING OF FLOWERS
Your arrangement will be seen to its best advantage if placed where the light can fall on it. If it is in a window with a light behind it, put it to one side, or near a lamp, because light and shade will make your vase look all the more exciting.

## TEXTURE AND COLOUR
Contrasting of colour, such as pussy willow with its brown stems and grey bobbles with some delicate fronds of ferns, would be striking against a pale almond green wall, for which vivid and bold groups the Dutch masterpieces by Van Huysum are well worth a study.

Always try and have a clear background; but at the same time it is fun to complement, perhaps, a picture, a piece of porcelain, a plate, an ornament or silver. Just imagine a vase of everlasting white sweet peas with grey foliage reflected in the light from a piece of silver.

## PRACTICAL POINTS
When you have gathered your flowers from the garden, or bought them from a shop, they will always benefit from a long drink, whether or not they have already been in water as is the case when buying from a shop. If any show signs of tiredness it is a good plan to use lukewarm water; sometimes hot water can be beneficial as in the case where hard-wooded materials such as guelder rose, lilac and chrysanthemums are used. Today there are several commercial types of chemicals in the form of crystals that will aid and prolong the life of many woody-stemmed shrubs and flowers.

It is a good plan when arranging flowers to fill the vase with warm water so that any air bubbles created in the stems while they were being cut will be dispersed. Some critics will say that all flowers do not like hot water, but my reply is that those that like it love it, and those that do not seem to put up with it remarkably well!

The whole *Helleborus* family are rather temperamental when used as a cut bloom; but they can last if they are given a long drink and placed in warm water up to their blooms for a good 24 hours. This is easily done by spreading a piece of 1·2 cm/½ in wire netting across the top of the bowl and placing the flowers through. Then put the flowers in your arrangement; but watch them, and if they wilt, take them out and give them the same treatment until they recover.

Lenten roses, *H. orientalis* also *H. argutifolius*, are another kettle of fish. There are several schools of thought on them. I prick them with a needle just under the head to disperse any air bubbles, and give them the same hot water treatment as mentioned in the previous paragraph. I like to pick *H. niger* when the stamens have just fallen and the suspicion of a seed pod is just forming; then you will find that they will last. *H. corsicus* is a late flowering variety which I will mention in a later chapter.

Twenty-four hours after arranging your flowers you will find that they have drunk quite a lot of water, so be sure and refill your vase and tubes after this time. After that, you will find that they drink less.

In the case of soft-stemmed and hollow-stemmed flowers, especially the ones that tend to decay under water such as the early summer flowers – bluebells, dahlias, asters, larkspur, etc, a few drops of a bleach in the water will help to stop the water discolouring and smelling. Everybody has their own tips with flowers such as lemonade for carnations, aspirins and copper coins for tulips, sugar for delphiniums and lilac, dipping poppies in hot wax, burning or singeing the stems of milky-stemmed flowers. I am strongly in favour of using any tip that will prolong the life of any flowers as these days they are expensive: a tip in time may save many a flower.

Another reminder to you is that flowers do like an airy room, but not draughts, so at night remove flowers to a cooler room if they are small enough to be carried, or else open a few windows to cool the room. Remember to shut the windows before retiring or you may find your flowers missing in the morning!

The arrangement for the cover is a display of yellow and orange late autumn flowers, some from my own garden and some bought from Covent Garden. It is arranged in the base of an old iron oil-lamp, and the flowers are held in place by a crumpled piece of wire netting. The flowers are yellow gerbera, *Lilium* 'Destiny', 'Enchantment' and 'Brandy Wine', antirrhinum, chrysanthemum, honeysuckle, protea the pincushion flower from South Africa with a head of white hydrangea. The foliage is golden privet, variegated ivy, camellia and *Garrya eliptica* When using mixed shades of all one colour, try and use as many shapes as possible.

# 3 Choosing and Buying Flowers

## FROM THE GARDEN

It is a happy experience for those who have a garden from which to pick, or who have the freedom of a kind friend's, as it provides far broader opportunities to find unusual leaves and flowers. As you walk around your eye may fall on some red beetroot leaves, a spray of clematis seed pods, red crab apples, an odd passion flower, or one or two stems of a late flowering pink everlasting sweet pea. One's fingers get positively itching to place them in a favourite vase. At the same time I am sure many flower arrangers feel the same as I do about the time it takes to do flowers from the garden. I myself take far longer when at home as I never seem to pick enough for the vase, and spend my time running backwards and forwards to the garden. However, I feel far happier to pick too few flowers rather than too many as I hate throwing any away; but still I find my kitchen windowsill is inevitably groaning under the weight of many a jam jar filled with leftovers. As I have said on a previous page, when doing a vase you normally list your flowers and foliage, therefore avoiding wastage; but it is a marvellous relaxation just to wander round the garden and look for unusual combinations.

One of my favourite arrangements last year was a rose bowl with five or six small blooms of the brown and yellow striped Rembrandt tulip, with several odd brown and yellow leaves of a grevillea that I had grown from seed several years ago, a few sprays of cream azalea, and some pinky brown trailing ivy leaves. This gave me a great thrill, not only from the actual arranging, but from the enjoyment of going round the garden looking for the various leaves and flowers that made up the vase. Try it this way and start off, say, with one pink flower, and go out and see how many matching things you can find to complete it. Don't miss out the vegetable patch or the weeds. That great gardener, A. E. Bowles, once said: 'There is no such thing as a weed; it is only a plant out of place'. This, I know, has been said in most other books on flower arranging, but it is true and I am very happy to repeat it here. In the same vein a garden correspondent in the *Country Life* magazine once said: 'It's nice to see a weed in the garden – it's friendly'. I must have the friendliest garden in Hertfordshire!

## BUYING FLOWERS

I have already talked about buying flowers from a shop, but to enlarge on that: visit your shop prepared with a list of your requirements, colouring, etc, at least a week beforehand so that you can see what is available. Then you can place an order, or go away and make a list knowing what the shop can get. You may have to buy your flowers over a period of days as some, such as lilies, usually arrive in bud and depending on the weather need a few days to come out; similarly with roses, paeonies, tulips, gladioli, etc. If you are arranging a bowl of paeonies or tulips it is a good idea to buy them over a period of days so that you have a combination of buds, open and half-open ones, giving your bowl a natural look just as though you had picked them from the garden. And remember to buy your flowers in good time so that they can have a long drink, also to give yourself the knowledge that you have them in your clutches; a flower in the hand is worth two on the shopping list! Nothing is more frustrating than to be unable to get the flowers you require, so buy early if you can. Most of my customers think that flowers grow on trees, and sometimes even think that I can produce their requirements out of thin air! Where possible I start organising my flowers at least two weeks before I need them so that if some are not available I can substitute others in place of the ones I had originally thought about.

Lilies in all shapes and sizes are, I think, most suitable for arranging, and if not grown at home in pots or in the garden, they are normally obtained from a shop. To begin with, I love them, and it distresses me that so many people dislike them.

25

Here we are looking down on an arrangement of mixed apricot and cream flowers suitable for a dining-room table. This was one of three arrangements designed for a beautiful room decorated in shades of yellow, a marvellous background for these colourings. The flowers used were *Lilium* 'Bonfire', orange carnations, cream single stocks, orange azalea blooms, Rembrandt tulips with two heads of *Lilium auratum*.

26

There is still this strong feeling against these lovely flowers; customers often murmur: 'Oh, they remind me of funerals'. In fact only the other day as I was arranging many stems of lilies along with other flowers for a City function, a passing waiter's comment was: 'Phew, it smells like dead bodies!' Quite often I have the request for no lilies at all, so I try to explain that there are more types of lilies than arums and *Lilium longiflorum* which are the two that are most used nowadays for weddings and so on. On the other hand lilies like *L. speciosum* 'Rubrum' and *L.* 'Corsage' are quite often taken for orchids! However there is such a galaxy of different varieties around from which to choose that I think it is worthwhile to mention by name a few which you can get today from the wholesale markets.

*L. longiflorum*, known as 'the white lily of florists' and usually prominent at weddings and funerals, is normally available all the year round.

*L. regale* is certainly one of the more popular and most used of the lilies, and is very easy to grow in the garden or in pots, May–June.

*L. speciosum* 'Rubrum' and *L. s.* 'Album' a lovely cascading lily, Turk's cap in shape, long-lasting in pink and white is again very easy to grow in pots or the garden blooming in late July or early August.

*L. auratum*, the golden-rayed lily of Japan. This is really superb, cream with a yellow throat and brown spots, long stemmed, and is marvellous for large arrangements; it has a heavy perfume.

*L. martagon*, quite a lovely Turk's cap-shaped lily, is marvellous for smaller arrangements, June flowering in a beautiful shade of mauve and in white.

*L.* 'Enchantment': This really is a most useful, long-lasting lily, very prolific in the garden or pots.

I have named just a few of my favourites and the most useful, but do try a few in your next arrangement. They are very worthwhile and will make all the difference with their various shapes, colour and texture.

# 4 Home Decoration

The purpose of arranging flowers for the house is to contribute an additional note of colour and happiness to our homes, and to my mind a room or house is not complete without the addition of a plant or flowers. The first thing I do when I get home is to go out into the greenhouse to find a plant, and then into the garden to pick a rose or two, just so that there is something in the house to tide over till I have time to concentrate on creating an arrangement. I do think fresh flowers around us take some of the strain out of our rushed lives.

When you are deciding upon your arrangements, do bear in mind the basic principles of design, balance and harmony. Remember that they must be complementary and fit into their surroundings to form an overall happy picture, not too large or too small, and in proportion to the positions in which you wish to put them, and that they should be in harmony with their surroundings.

One easy way to arrange flowers for the home is to make a mixed vase. Pop out into the garden and cut whatever you see in bloom, and group them together in complementary colouring. It's rather fun sometimes to see how many flowers can be used successfully in an arrangement.

One of my favourite colourings is apricot cream through to green. In June I would use for height Suttons' apricot foxgloves, for centre interest a garden rose called 'Apricot Nectar' for sidelines, *Lilium regale*, filling in *Alchemilla mollis* and variegated hosta leaves with foliage of stripped lime.

## SPRING

Spring brings to mind your first snowdrop, or a spray of

wintersweet or hamamelis (witch hazel), a spray of either of which will perfume a room. As the first of the year's flowers start one is loath to pick many, so it is a good idea to keep a good supply of house plants which you can use as additional material for your arrangement. A few crocus blooms can be enhanced by a small ivy, a *Hedera canariensis*, *Begonia rex* or a small fern plant in a flat dish with a piece of drift wood to hide the pots. This is also the time when you can appreciate the flowering bulbs grown indoors during the winter months, which were planted in early October. Do find nice shallow bowls or baskets with metal linings. Old vegetable dishes are ideal, or you can grow the bulbs in boxes and then move them at the right moment. In the case of hyacinths this is when the flower is showing above the leaves. You can then plant them on meat dishes, and with the addition of a fern or two, a few small rocks, and a moss-covered branch, you can show them off to advantage. Later, you can add other flowering plants and bulbs to this dish, thereby assuring yourself of weeks of pleasure.

The bulbs of hyacinth 'Borah' make a very pleasing show over a long period; they come in shades of pink, blue and white. Miniature narcissi are ideal to add to your plate garden. Then they can all be put back and grown on again in the garden for another year. But do remember to spray them with a foliar feed after they have finished flowering as this will build up the flowers for the next year.

**Bedroom Flowers** Flowers are always a warm and welcoming sight in a guest's bedroom. Choose a side table or dressing table to place them on, perhaps using a china figurine or a pretty cup and saucer filled with forget-me-nots, small fragrant flowers, jasmine, sweet peas, snowdrops in a Bristol blue finger bowl, or a little posy of all your smaller flowers looking like a tapestry pin cushion.

**Hall Flowers** These are very important as the hall vase is usually the first one to be seen. Use a heavy type of vase because the hall, being a very much used passage with people walking past and doors opening, makes the vase very vulnerable to being knocked over.

**Living Room Flowers** Avoid using too many flower vases in one room. A tall vase or a pedestal arrangement, together with a low vase on an occasional table, is really enough in a fairly large room. I think another good plan is to have a mixed vase, and another of all one flower or colour to complement the larger mixed one.

**Plants** A brief note on plants: it is always a good idea to have them in the house standing on various shelves or window sills. But also try collecting them altogether in one group; this can look equally attractive with each plant complementing the others.

### TABLE FLOWERS

The first and most important thing to remember about flowers for a table is that they must be low enough so as not to interfere with the diners' view of each other. Secondly, the table arrangement should be attractive from every angle from which it is seen; the only exception is buffet flowers which are usually seen from the front. There is no need to fill the vase with a symmetrical arrangement of flowers to make it perfect from all angles. When constructing your arrangement, try using lacy flowers for the ends and your choice low-growing blooms for the centre, with one or two pretty leaves to pull it all together. Remember to sit at the table and see if there are any gaps or wire netting showing; but do show a little of the container, especially if it is silver or a piece of pretty china, as it helps to break the line of solid flowers. Colouring is usually determined by the decorations of the room, but a good idea is to try a gradual shading of all one colour such as 'Apricot Nectar' roses, coral gerberas, montbretia, sweet peas with apricot stocks, for foliage use leaves of tellima just tinged with brown of autumn, and pale green alchemilla can be used for filling in.

Arrangements for tables should be made giving thought to the overall effect, taking into account that garden flowers in a pottery bowl would look well on a hessian-type table cloth with an informal table setting, whereas a table setting of the formal type with crystal and silver would need more exotic flowers.

This is a blend of mixed yellow and green foliages with yellow and white flowers, the dominating flowers being the white antirrhinum; to show them off I surrounded them with the green 'Rayonnant' chrysanthemum. The next shapes I used were the creamy trumpets of *Lilium auratum*, the golden-rayed Lily of Japan, together with *Lilium* 'Destiny' and the sprays of white euphorbia foliage; the clear yellow gerberas pulled the whole arrangement together. The background of foliage was of golden privet with two large leaves of monstera to give a feeling of depth. A large pottery *tazza* was used and again I used wire netting to hold the arrangement together.

31

Luncheon flowers can be an arrangement of fruit with perhaps several leaves with one or two flowers tucked in amongst them, or a bowl of globe artichokes with their own leaves, and a bunch of purple grapes in a low wicker basket or wooden bowl. Or perhaps a small pottery jug of fiery orange nasturtiums with their own leaves would add colour on an early autumn day. A more exotic combination could be of peaches with a small pineapple, and as a finishing touch stephanotis blooms tucked in around the fruit. Submerge the stephanotis flowers in water for half an hour before use, as this will keep them fresh for several hours.

Many years ago white damask table cloths used to be *de rigueur*, but now we have a variety of surfaces: glass, wood, and a marvellous selection of materials to make special table cloths. In recent years felt has become most used for special events; it has a lovely texture and comes in such a wealth of colours which are perfect foils for flowers. For a summer party I made round table cloths of apple green felt, with throw-over squares of white nylon, the curtain variety, and had low bowls of white daisies with a white candle which gave a lovely impression of simplicity and coolness. For another party I was able to dispense with the white table cloth and had garlands of red and apricot autumn flowers with mixed berries around a silver candlestick. Old wine glasses can be used to show off fragrant stems of jasmine or sprays of *Clematis montana*. Do have a hunt around for unusual containers. One of my favourites is a silver sugar bowl with a Bristol blue lining which looks delightful full of snowdrops.

When confronted by a large table for a dinner it is best to vary the arrangements. So, for example, start with a long arrangement, then a bowl, etc; it will break the line so as not to give an over-solid effect. I remember once when I was asked to arrange flowers for a banquet and the table was 44 m/144 ft long and 2 m/7 ft wide! I decided to use mixed sweet peas and beforehand I worked it out on graph paper as the butler wished to use several pieces of silver. I used the same technique as I have just mentioned in the previous sentence – started with a lacy arrangement with a bowl in between. The effect was riveting; that was five years ago and people still remember it. Not all arrangements are as easy as that. When I was arranging flowers in a government building in London, the host had obtained from a Royal Horticultural Society show 70 stems of a special rose for the table because of a 70th birthday of someone who shared the same name as the rose. Unfortunately they were all only 15 cm/6 in long! But with the help of velvety *Begonia rex* leaves, and trails of *Rosa rubrifolia* foliage, we saved the situation.

In other chapters I have mentioned various other table arrangements under their special headings.

A marquee in blue and white arranged in all white flowers. The central pole had first attached to it two oasis blocks covered with 2·5 cm/1 in wire netting, then the flowers were pushed into it to create the appearance of a hanging basket. Small similar arrangements were also used on the walls at regular intervals. Blue ribbon was used to flow out of the bouquets to tie in with the theme. To finish we used glass lanterns with white candles with the base surrounded by white flowers. The flowers used were white marguerites with single spray chrysanthemums. The foliage used was *Senecio greyii* and grey eucalyptus.

# 5 Party Arrangements

## CHRISTMAS

Christmas to my mind is made up of a variety of smells, besides that of the turkey, of course. It is a time for evergreen foliage: ilex, the holly, both the green and the variegated, pine and larch cones, and candles. These, made up into garlands can also include apples and tangerines, and may be made to hang with red ribbon either by the fireplace or on any vacant piece of wall. When thinking where to position your decorations, it is a good idea to come in through the front door and see where you look first – perhaps at a table or a blank space of wall. Similarly do this in every room in which you wish to place decorations; it will help you in creating a pattern and concentration of your arrangements whilst still imparting a festive air. I have always been of the opinion that it is better to have one superb decoration in a room rather than lots of small, insignificant ones dotted around.

To return to the garlands or swags: these are best done on thick sisal-type string. Measure the length you require, plus a bit extra as it is inclined to shrink, then knot it at one end. Take your materials (eg blue pine, larch cones on twigs, apples and tangerines). Wire the larch cones, apples and tangerines, and also one or two pieces of blue pine. This is because you are going to shape the end of the garland, which many people forget to do. Wire used is $20 \times 10$ gauge which you can obtain at most florists. Start by shaping the end, and once you have done this, bind the blue pine in together with the wired larch cones and fruit. To each 30cm/12in use three apples, good shiny ones, and two tangerines. Finish off with a big bow of red ribbon with long ribbon trails. If you wish to do this either side of a fireplace you can make a joining swag across the top, starting thinly from the ends culminating in a large centre. Remember to start the return end wiring the other way, away from the centre.

Having talked about using fresh materials, one must not pass by the useful artificial materials you can find which come under the heading of gum and glitter; they are so useful because they can be arranged in advance. Fortunately today you can buy some really pretty leaves and flowers already glittered as opposed to the old days when you had to do it yourself. A pretty idea for a hall table or a corner is to get a large, well-shaped branch and tie small arrangements of leaves and flowers shaped like small bouquets along it at intervals. The number of intervals depends on the branch and the amount of space you have. The branch can be nailed on to a wooden base, placed in a shallow container, and held in place by gilded or silvered bricks or stones to hide the mechanics.

Whilst we are on this subject, another quick and attractive idea is to get a well-shaped birch branch with its catkins on, and cover it with spider webs made of fuse wire sprinkled with silver glitter. These can be made on a board with a nail in the centre and then a circle of seven nails. This is a time for children, so a seasonal idea for them, and not at all costly, is to find a nice looking log with perhaps some moss on, then get an earthenware flower pot and stick it on with some Polyfilla. Water the Polyfilla down to a dropping consistency and pour over the top of the flower pot to resemble a fall of snow. Take an artificial robin and stick it on the top of the pot, then embellish log and pot with trails of ivy, and sprigs of holly with tips touched with liquid Pollyfilla to look like snow.

For the dining table, which is usually the *pièce de résistance*, there is nothing to outshine a collection of *Helleborus niger*, (Christmas rose) sprigs of variegated holly, winter jasmine and ivy trails set in a silver basket with a hoop of holly leaves and fir circling the arrangement. The hellebores are notorious for not flowering in time for Christmas unless it is exceptionally mild. I find that if you dig up the whole plant and place it in a greenhouse two or three weeks before you need them, beautifully clean blooms will come up on lovely long stems. This does not seem to harm the plant, but rather rejuvenates it; each year as I dig up the same plant, it seems to flower more than in the previous years.

Christmas, being a major church festival, calls for traditional arrangements of evergreen foliage such as gaultheria, leucothoe, camellias, and holly in all forms. There are some lovely yellow berried varieties, silver and golden leafed as well as weeping ones. As flowers are expensive and difficult to find at this time of the year it is a good idea to use the poinsettia plant to go with the evergreens. Instead of cutting it, which means burning and waxing the ends to keep it from drooping, use the whole plant in the arrangement either by propping it up with the foliage or, a better idea, pushing small bamboo canes up through the base of the plant, using the drainage holes, then placing the plant with the canes into the arrangement where it will be held firm by the wire netting.

To help your foliage to preserve its freshness give it a good drink before cutting for arrangements, and spray with leaf shine which can be obtained from most florists or plant centres. For small arrangements it is fun going round the garden or hedgerows to find sprays of hazel catkins, wild rose hips, ivy with its black fruits of ivy turned pink with the cold, little sprigs of pine, odd clusters of mistletoe which, all sprayed with leaf shine and placed in a bowl or vase, with the addition of a stem or two of chincherinchee (the South African wind flower – as the wind rustles through the paper thin flowers it is heard to call the sound 'chincherinchee') or a couple of *Helleborus niger*, would grace any table at the festive season.

To touch on Christmas trees, which to my mind are a 'must' at Christmas, if you are starting afresh with no handed-down ornaments as most families seem to have, try decorating the tree in a colour scheme. Red and white is an effective one with little white lights, stars made of gingerbread and iced white and tied on with thin red ribbon, small red and white crackers, and red baubles. Another suggestion is to spray pine cones gold and have gold lights, crackers and baubles. There are endless possibilities and schemes in which you and the family can join together.

### HALLOWE'EN
Flowerwise, marvellous fun can be had on this occasion to

create an evening of magic and fun. Pumpkins can be used to great advantage for decoration, especially after having made a rather delectable soup from the flesh (see below). Just in case any of you are interested in cooking, as I am myself, I include this recipe. I have always found that the majority of people who can cook can arrange flowers, and this reminds me of an occasion when I was asked to broadcast on a BBC programme whilst on holiday. The interviewer said that she could not cook; I answered that therefore she was probably no good at arranging flowers? She acknowledged that that was a fact. I have seen her several times since, but have yet to be asked to do another broadcast on flowers!

### Cream of Pumpkin and Shrimp soup
Peel a 2lb slice of pumpkin, throw away the seeds and the cottony centre, cut the flesh into small pieces, salt and pepper them, and put them into a thick saucepan with a stick of celery cut in pieces. Cover them with $1\frac{1}{2}$ pints of milk previously boiled, and one pint of mild stock or water, simmer until the pumpkin is tender, about 30 minutes. Sieve the mixture; return the purée to a clean pan. Mash or pound shrimps in a mortar; 4oz of peeled prawns or shrimps will do (or potted shrimps), adding a few drops of lemon juice. Dilute with a little of the pumpkin purée, add this mixture to the soup, simmer gently for ten minutes or so, sieve again if the soup is not quite smooth, taste for seasoning and, when reheating, thin with a little more hot milk or stock if necessary. Immediately before serving stir in a good lump of butter. Ample for six.

After that little *divertissement* let us get back to pumpkins. You can take the two halves of the pumpkin and proceed to cut a face out of each; then fix a night light inside the shells. If you hang them against a piece of black material or a black painted panel they make handsome wall decorations; or even one on your front door would make a welcome feature for the start of your party.

Now for other arrangements: this is where fruit could be used together with late autumn flowers and hedgerow fruits. A decoration of a pyramid of fruits for the centre of a buffet

38

Summer banquet is represented here in this arrangement of cream, apricot and salmon flowers. The idea came as I looked at the rather beautiful painting by Jan Breughel of a garden scene. I did not want to compete with the painting, but wanted to related to it in its softness of texture. I therefore used a simple low china cache-pot and arranged a flowering collection of grey-green foliage consisting of angelica heads, white *Astrantia maxima*, *Eryngium tripartitum* before it turned blue, alchemilla, and trails of ballota. The *Lilium auratum* made a central focal point, and an outline of *Lilium* 'African Queen' gave a framework for some lovely stems of rose 'Apricot Nectar'. The star-shaped quality of the salmon gerberas gave a subtle interest; fuchsia leaves gave a feeling of depth.

39

is a good idea, giving you maximum room on the table and also giving height to your buffet table. You need a good, deep, urn-shaped vase, deep enough in which to place a stick for roughly 23 cm/9 in so that it will support the cone of wire netting and moss that you are going to place on top. Cut yourself a large piece of 2·5 cm/1 in mesh wire netting about 1 m/3 ft long and 60 cm/2 ft wide, shape it into a cone and put the thin end into the vase, taking in less moss as you get to the top. Squeeze it into shape, making a thin cone as your fruit will stick out. Leave a 10 cm/4 in piece of stick free from the moss to support your top fruit. Collect your mixture of fruit: apples (windfalls will do to fill in, but get one or two red, shiny ones for the front), grapes (good for shape, especially the seedless ones), bananas, lemons, tangerines, melons, and water melons cut as slices are particularly effective, and pine-apples (the baby ones cut in half go further), one of which should have a leafy top for the top of your cone. Spread your fruit over the mossed cone by using thick wires 35 × 50 cm/ 14 × 20 in and passing them through the fruits. When you have got the basic shape fill in the spaces with pale green hydrangea, parsley or alchemilla, clusters of sweet chestnuts in their green shells, or horse chestnuts which are particularly eye-catching if left in the shells with a section missing. Finish with a collar of wired ivy or camellia leaves. Remember that after the party all the fruits can be used for a fruit salad.

A pyramid of vegetables, which is great fun, can also be made; or you could have two pyramids, one of fruit and the other of vegetables. You can make fruit and flower wall hangings just as effectively by using a flat baton with pads of moss. Take the flat baton and attach three pads of moss, which you have bound together with string, and tie them on to the baton. Place a hook on the top of the baton so that you can hang it on to a rail or picture hook. Then on each pad place your wired fruit, flowers and leaves in an attractive design in the manner of that great wood carver, Grinling Gibbons; connect the three with a suitable coloured ribbon with a bow at the top. Try and find long-lasting flowers as they will need to be out of water for quite a time. You can make this type of garland the day before and, after you have finished it, remove the flowers and put them in a bowl of water to keep them fresh. Types of flowers that can be used are any type of lily, chrysanthemums, carnations, gerberas, anthirrinums; shiny leaves: camellias, codiaeums, ivy; fruits: grapes, artichokes, bananas, lemons. Many a pleasant hour can be had looking at church and house carvings to glean ideas. I once visited Waddesdon Manor near Newbury in Berkshire and there, in one of the rooms, are four marvellous carvings. It is well worth a visit, and it certainly gave me ideas.

## EASTER

Easter brings to mind the crown imperial fritillaries which grow in the garden and always come into bloom at that time. They are alleged to have grown at the foot of the Cross, and as you turn the flower upwards you can see the five tears of the Virgin Mary. There is a lot of history or folklore about various flowers, and as I have always found this interesting, I will include as much as possible in the various chapters. Plant these lilies on their sides, and remember that they do not like being moved. Whenever digging near the spot, you will notice their pungent aroma exuding from the ground. Be careful when using them in the house as they still give out that same aroma, and if you have not told anybody about this, you will find your friends hunting around to try and discover from where the smell can be coming.

Another delightful decoration is a garden made on an old meat dish or a large plate. This is where a few small house plants will come in useful: little ferns, ivies, peperomias. Put in your dish a few crocks and, if available, a few pieces of charcoal. Sprinkle with a little soil, then place your plants in a pleasing design mixing them with a few flowering ones such as a polyanthus or baby daffodils which can be dug from the garden and then returned. A primula would give a little height; a mirror could form a little pond with one or two attractive stones from the garden, together with a small log over which you could trail your ivy. Then take some green moss and place all over the soil area pinning it on with $25 \times 10\,\text{cm}/10 \times 4\,\text{in}$ wires bent into the shape of a hairpin. Make a little path of pebbles using a broken flower pot crushed up into chippings. Later on you could include a small glass pot filled with one or two cut flowers; endless possibilities are open to you. A plate

This novelty was created for a birthday party as a centre piece for a buffet table. The host was born under the sign of 'Pisces' so the central theme was to be the sign of the two fishes. The basic shape was made of sphagnum moss shaped into the fish shape with an outer covering of 2·5 cm/1 in mesh wire netting to hold the moss, and the flowers and leaves when pinned on by wire pins–in fact, just like hair pins. First we looked for a scale-looking fruit or flower, so we used artichoke fruits. The fins were the flower of *Pieris formosa*, which have these creamy white panicles rather like lily-of-the-valley flowers. The lips were of beetroot and the mouth of red carnation petals. The tail and large fins were leaves of the house plant dieffenbachia and the surrounds of the eyes were petals of *Lilium* 'Enchantment'. It was held by a bent metal rod disguised with water reeds to create a feeling of movement.

To complement the fish made for the Piscean Party were wall hangings of fruit and flowers. Down a 1·5 m/5 ft piece of wood were placed three bricks of moss surrounded by 2·5 cm/1 in wire netting. The display was made up of bananas, green grapes, artichokes, green peppers and lemons. The flowers were *Lilium* 'Green Dragon' with yellow gerberas. The wooden batten was hidden by yellow ribbon, and the whole wall drop was finished by the addition of ribbon bows. On each table glass lanterns were arranged with a surround of yellow ranunculus and alchemilla.

garden such as this is so useful when flowers are scarce, and afterwards you still have the green plants for another year. If you are good at modelling you could make a shape of a rabbit out of wire, tie on the moss thinly with string, then pin on small flowers with silver wire gauge 32 hairpins. Use wallflowers or primroses, with the black centres of anemones for the eyes and nose and silver wires for the whiskers, and finish off with a ribbon round its neck. Similarly you could make an Easter egg of flowers sitting on a meat dish covered with green moss and small posies of spring flowers which could be given as little presents to your family and friends. You could also have great fun with Jemima Puddleduck, making the shape with moss then pinning on white tulip petals which have the texture and look of feathers, and use yellow daffodil petals for the beak and feet. It is sometimes difficult to make eyes out of flowers, so borrow Teddy's eyes, or pop into a shop and buy some doll's eyes. A little cape out of material and a bonnet would make this an ideal centrepiece for a children's Easter party.

Children love a centrepiece so, at whatever time of the year, a maypole made of coloured ribbon, with a small posy of flowers at each point of the ribbon, could be colourful and gay. Make a crown out of gold foil to go around the top, and under it place a collar of tiny flowers with perhaps the initial of the person whose party it is. With the little spray of flowers the place name could be attached, and then a game could ensue to guess the names of the flowers at each place, and a small prize could be given. The ribbon used can be of the 2·5 cm/1 in waterproof sort available at most flower shops and plant centres.

## HOSPITAL FLOWERS

It is a good idea to gather a small mixed posy of flowers from the garden if possible and place it in a container so that nurses do not have to be bothered for a vase. As there is never much room, make it small so that people can have it beside them; it is also more personal if smaller. In your posy try and find one or two flowers which will take time to open; nothing is more tranquillising and pleasing than to watch a flower come into bloom. Do not take a flower which has too strong a scent because in a small area it can become overpowering. Another thing to watch is not to take mixed red and white flowers as there is a superstition that they are unlucky.

## VALENTINE'S DAY

The Church Synod has declared that this feast should be discontinued as they have discovered that St Valentine never existed. However, the custom is harmless and gives great pleasure to many, and it is a chance to try your skill at a flower Valentine. Take a small block of oasis and cut it in half, then cut the shape of a heart. Get a collection of small flowers– violets, grape hyacinths–and a small pointed stick to make holes in the oasis. Place the flower buds in a pattern of the heart in circles, finishing off with a rosebud. To keep the flowers fresh, back the oasis part of the heart with silver tinfoil to keep in the moisture.

## ANNIVERSARIES

On anniversaries a posy of flowers or a corsage are especially appreciated, so try making a corsage yourself. You will need first from the florist some vase wires, gauge 32, a roll of gutta percha (plastic film) and a reel of silver wire gauge 32. Then take three roses and two buds. The roses should have their stems cut off quite close to the flower's head. The less stem you leave, the neater the finished product. The wire is pushed into the calyx, twisted round the short stem twice, and then covered with the gutta percha. Twist the gutta percha round where the wire was pushed in, hold it with your fingers, and then twirl the stem bringing the tape down to the end of the wire. Wire and cover each of the roses and buds. Then, using either the rose leaves or ivy leaves, wire these with the 32 silver wire pushing the wire through the middle of the leaf drawing both ends down, hairpin style, and twisting them round the stem.

On a spray of rose leaves, only the top leaf need be wired. Cover with gutta percha. Then take the roses and buds and separate them into two clusters, with three roses going one way and two the other. Wire the two clusters together in the middle, add the leaves, and bend them into an attractive design.

This charming drawing room, decorated in a haze of blue, was the ideal setting for a massed summer arrangement. Standing in front of a window it needed to have a strong outline of foliage to throw up the soft colourings. The foliage used was *Atriplex rubra*, with its deep crimson leaves and purplish flowers, and forsythia foliage. Amongst the flowers were *Lilium* 'Destiny', *L. speciosum* 'Rubrum' yellow gerberas pink dahlias, belladonna lily and tall stems of *Eupatorium purpureum*. The vase used was a marble *tazza*.

46

## BUFFET FLOWERS

With this type of decoration you can really let yourself go with all kinds of ideas. No one will be sitting at the table, but, at the same time, remember that the flowers must be away from the food so as to enhance the table and not create a muddled layout. Use a tall vase with a tall, spreading, or fan-shaped arrangement, or you can make a pyramid of fruits and leaves. One of the more unusual and attractive decorations for a buffet would be a tree of flowers, the construction of which I have described in the chapter on Christmas decorations. In the summer white marguerites with grasses and alchemilla are light and pretty. The autumn brings us apricot dahlias with berried shrubs, winter brings variegated holly, scarlet carnations, and festive red ribbons which could be used to decorate the front of the buffet. Mimosa heralds the spring, and there are countless themes to think up. The tree is very practical in that it rises up off the table and can be seen by all your friends even when they are standing.

A cornucopia of hydrangeas is easy to make on a wire frame covered with moss; this filled with fruit cascading on to the table it would make a fitting centre piece for a harvest supper. In a fruit arrangement your principal problem is to use the form of the fruits artistically. Pineapples, pumpkins, water melons are the heavy fruits for the basic form of the arrangement. Remember when using a water melon it looks most effective when a slice has been removed and it is used with the smaller fruits. Apples, oranges, avocados, pears, grapes are the smaller types of fruit. Group them just as though arranging a vase, placing the oranges next to the green, the purples to highlight the apricots. If using bananas keep them together; do not spread them around like pebbles on a beach. To unite them all, take large glossy leaves like fig or fatsia seed heads, sweet chestnut fruits, and a trail or two of the passion flower, and after the arrangement has fulfilled its purpose, it's fruit salad for a week!

For a simple garden or barbecue party use a collection of vegetables in the same manner in a trug basket or a large wooden bowl which, placed on a hessian tablecloth, would certainly look attractive. When using fruits or vegetables, do give them a good polish so that they shine.

## WALL VASES

These are most suitable when the flower space is at a premium. Containers can be from straw hats hung with ribbon to wicker shopping baskets, the type that old fashioned fishmongers used. I have seen silver food covers cut in half. (My teeth are still on edge since I first saw them used!) Blocks of oasis are good, inexpensive, and simple to construct with the aid of 2·5 cm/1 in mesh wire netting to hold them together. I once used for a young persons' party Wellington boots which are marvellous for holding water. I sprayed them with gold paint, and hung them on the wall with yellow carnations and grasses sprawling out of them. On another occasion I used some old leather army boots, sprayed silver, with white ribbon laces. I filled them with white heather and used them on board a ship for a wedding party.

The great joy of wall hangings is that you can create all kinds of interesting ideas with odd containers, so hunt around in junk shops and garden sheds to find just the thing to use.

Try looking in books or in churches at the work of Grinling Gibbons, one of our greatest wood carvers, specialising in garlands of fruit and flowers; he will start you on many a new idea. Make a collection of old garden forks and spades, paint them white, add some bunches of corn, seed pods, leaves, and then add a watering can, painted white, to fill in the centre. Use a few sprays of chrysanthemums or dahlias in a block of oasis to keep the foliage and flowers fresh. Add a few trails of old man's beard, and you have built yourself a good wall centrepiece.

Alternatively, take a 1·7 m/5½ ft batten of wood, place three nails at intervals along the wood, and attach three half-blocks of oasis, which have been covered by 2·5 cm/1 in mesh wire netting, on to the nails. Then hang it on a suitable wall, either from the picture rail or a picture hook. Take a collection of leaves and fruits and place them in a pleasing arrangement. Finish off with a long ribbon, starting with a bow from the top, and use the ribbon to connect each display to the other, at the same time covering the wood.

When next you go into a room, look not only to see where you can place a vase, but also at the walls to see where you could perhaps hang a wall drop of fruits and flowers.

48

## PARTY TABLES

If you are giving a larger type of party, and if you are having round tables, you could cover them with different coloured cloths, using a separate flower to match the cloth. A green cloth would look lovely with a collection of green leaves and seed pods, a mauve table with mauve sweet peas or fuchsias, a white cloth with white daisies, and so forth; you could then seat your guests at the rose table or the fuchsia table. If it is the time of year when flowers are plentiful, try making the trees I have described for the buffet table in a previous chapter for each table. They would be tall enough for your friends to be able to chat under them, and also give you more room on the table for glasses, and so on.

Where vases are not able to be used, wall hangings really come into their own. These cascades of sweet peas and ferns held by ribbon streamers were placed at intervals round the walls of a ballroom. They were constructed from a large batten of wood with bricks of oasis foam placed at intervals.

# 6 Church Flowers

**WEDDING FLOWERS**

This is a time when flowers play an all-important part of the day. They can take up the colouring of the bridesmaids' dresses or even the flowers that they carry, and whether it be a large town church or a small country one, keep the flowers simple, effective, and placed in the most advantageous positions so that they can be seen by all, remembering that the church will be full of people standing throughout most of the service.

Before the flowers are to be arranged in the church, it is not only polite but advisable to contact the vicar, verger or flower organiser to ascertain exactly where the church authorities like the flowers to be placed. Most churches leave it to your discretion; but some like them on the altar, and some do not, while others have definite ideas which they prefer you to adhere to. I have nearly always found that if the bride or bride's mother would like flowers in a particular position, a little diplomatic chat with all concerned works wonders.

Before you go to do your arranging, it is important to remember to ask where the water supply is, and also about any services that might take place. Once, not having checked this, I found myself arranging flowers for a wedding in an out-of-the-way country church, and whilst working, I noticed that, one by one, several people came in and sat down. I thought to myself how nice of the villagers to take so much interest in the flowers for the local wedding, but to my astonishment, in fifteen minutes I had quite a congregation. My previous self-flattering thoughts were rudely shattered when someone

51

came up to me and asked if I knew that there was to be a funeral service in just a few minutes? I swept all the flowers to one side and hastily vanished, hoping that the half-done flowers would perhaps be a comfort on a sad day. So the moral is, do check a few days prior to your going to the church.

I have found in my experience that to arrange the flowers the day before gives them time to settle; and possibly yourself, too, should you be attending the wedding as a guest. This leaves plenty of time on the day to arrange the flowers for wherever the reception is being held. Remember to pop into the church to top up the vases, and metal tubes if used, with water. Never try and do both the church and reception on the same day, unless it means only a vase in each place, as it is too frustrating for yourself and the bride if you are rushing around at the last moment trying to get finished. I think it is nice if you can do it this way as it will possibly give the bride a chance to see the arrangements. So often on 'The Day', between the veil and tears, she does not have much time to take it all in, or to appreciate the beauty of the flowers and all the hard work entailed.

## ALTAR FLOWERS
Most churches have their own vases which have, no doubt, been presented by an individual as a memorial, or by the Mothers' Union, the Guild, etc, which they like to be used. No doubt they will be of the narrow-necked, carafe type which makes it almost impossible to arrange flowers in a graceful manner. The way round this is to take your wire netting and squash it into the vase, leaving about 10cm/4in above the rim; then put in about three small metal tubes which will be held by this support of wire netting. This will increase your flower space, and indeed gives you a chance to make a creditable display.

Keep the altar simple when choosing the flowers. The longiflorum lilies, being many-headed, and white with a greenish white line in the centre of the trumpet, lend them-selves admirably to small vases; or, on the simpler side, daisies with their thin stems look fresh and countrified. Sometimes a low arrangement in front of the cross on an altar, especially if there are candles, goes to make a central

52

focal point, and it will look especially good if there are two vases either side of the church steps. I advocate all one type of flower for the altar; it is usually most effective as there is greater scope for a mixed collection for the other flowers in the church.

## CHANCEL FLOWERS AND PEDESTAL GROUPS

These are often arranged on pedestals; most churches have their own pedestals and sometimes their own vases to go with them. If no vases, which are expensive to buy and difficult to find, the good old china wash basins, picked up at a junk shop or bazaar and painted gold or black, make ideal containers. Painted enamel wash basins also look very fine on black wrought-iron stands.

In choosing the flowers you can now pick on the colour scheme, perhaps taking into account the colour of the bridesmaids' dresses or the flowers that they will be carrying, or maybe tie up with the bride's mother's outfit, or even the bride's favourite colour. If none of these ideas are forthcoming, then perhaps you can pick on a colour which will suit the church, taking in the surroundings and furnishings, ie stained glass windows, carpets, altar hangings, or even the time of year: yellow and white for Easter, pinks and white for early summer, coral and apricot for the autumn. Try to keep the flowers on the bright and airy side.

Starting with the spring flowers, the early cherry blossom, especially the dark bronze leaf variety with the pinky-blue flowers, which incidentally I think was China's greatest gift to the rest of the world, if forced, really surprises you as it will produce pale green leaves and palest pink flowers of tissue paper texture. Mix this with the forced viburnum guelder rose, stems of *Euphorbia wulfenii* of the spurge family, sprigs of the early *Rhododendron* 'Christmas Cheer', and some pale yellow tulips, 'Ossi Oswalda' or 'Mothers' Day', together with some leaves of *Cynara cardunculus*, the cardoon, with its great arching silver leaves, boldy cut which will give the arrangement a central feature. This will surely give the bride the greatest of joy and pleasure with the minimum amount of cost.

The late spring brings us a wealth of material to use. A vase

This flower tree was one of a pair decorating the entrance of a hotel which was the venue for a wedding. As it was a summer wedding, these trees were made to give a feeling of summer coolness. The flowers used were white marguerites, single spray *Chrysanthemum* 'Bonnie Jean', white carnations with green grey foliage. The construction of the trees was 2m/7ft pole fixed into a wooden garden tub and weighted by several building bricks. On top of the pole were placed two bricks of oasis wrapped round with 2·5cm/1in mesh wire netting.

of all-white flowers, with palest grey foliage, looks simply lovely against the stone background of a church. Using the foliage whitebeam of the *Sorbus* family, again the cynara leaves, or cardoon as it is called, *Senecio greyii*, trails of *Hedera canariensis variegata* with white lilac stripped off its leaves, sprigs of *Spiraea* 'Bridal Wreath' (a very appropriate name for a wedding), double white tulips 'Tacoma', longiflorum lilies with some heads of an early white rhododendron with leaves removed, will give you a good mass effect for the centre of your arrangement.

A word about the stripping of foliage from shrubs and trees. This is a good idea as you expose the flowers for effect, and dispense with the heaviness of the leaves. Lilac lasts longer if the leaves are removed, and guelder rose looks more effective without the leaves around the green/white baubles. Lime trees are a particular asset when stripped to show off their pale green wings. I read in one of Constance Spry's early books how Queen Alexandra, when she was Princess of Wales, first started the fashion of placing branches of foliage in vases. I sometimes have occasion to go to Marlborough House, now the official Commonwealth entertaining palace, and I stand and wonder if her late Majesty knew what she had started.

Rhododendrons are more effective if the leaves are removed from around the flowers, and horse chestnut, too, will last longer if stripped of leaves. Some very dear friends of mine were married in chestnut time at a cathedral church in the country. Chestnut branches with their flowers were being used and the leaves were stripped by the arrangers in the church. The nuns, who usually did the flowers themselves, were avidly watching, and the story goes that, for many years afterwards, not a leaf was to be seen on a branch of flowers, so taken were they by the idea! This is why I have listed some flowers and foliage which lend themselves to this treatment. One or two more to be added to the ones I have mentioned are sycamore with their green and bronze seed pods or wings for autumn use, and wych elm which is particularly good as it does it itself! Or, I should say, it has its lovely pale green wings before the leaves appear – very sensible! Remember it takes time to strip leaves off a branch, so try doing what you require for your vases several days earlier.

To return to the placing of the flowers in a church: one arrangement in a prominent position is more effective than a number scattered about the place. A large church has its own problems, so do not try and compete with the masonry or the carvings and fabrics, but place the vases in the most suitable positions looking for a solid and suitable background such as by the pulpit or lectern, or maybe either side of the altar, somewhere where all the guests can see them. Use light colours for a dark church, but be careful with the reds and blues which are apt to disappear, and use pale blush pinks with the reds, white, cream and yellows to show off blue. Also try and find a position where a light will fall on your group. Not all churches have good lighting as it is such an expensive item today, but it certainly makes a world of difference to a group of flowers if they are lit up, or placed somewhere where the natural light can fall on them.

In small country churches wild flowers can look very effective, but a certain control must be used or the final effect will be messy. Cow parsley, or Queen Anne's lace, was first used with great success by Mrs Spry, and subsequently by nearly everyone else who has had the opportunity of decorating a country church. I do find a little goes a long way, but used on its own, or with grasses and daisies, together with a couple of more formal arrangements, it will give a pleasing effect. Not always is cow parsley acceptable, it seems. A friend, whose turn it was on the Sunday flower roster in her little Wiltshire church which, incidentally, was surrounded by hedgerows of cow parsley, arranged her vase with just that and decorative cabbage leaves. She found herself removed from the list for some years! So moderation in all things; but no doubt a London wedding organiser would have been delighted with a touch of the country.

Later on in the year apricot and cream can look lovely as autumn approaches, with the foliage just turning colour. Try using azalea, horse chestnut, parrotia foliage, apricot gladioli, the cream with brown spots of *Lilium auratum* which is the golden rayed lily of Japan, pale green hydrangea for the centre, tassels of green love-lies-bleeding, *Amaranthus caudatus* 'Alba', and the dahlia 'Sugar Time', with one or two of the lovely single chrysanthemum 'Olnura'.

56

Again, as winter approaches, the pale grey of eucalyptus as a background, some arching stems of variegated holly, late hydrangea with its pale blue and green, and the single chrysanthemum daisies 'Bonnie Jean', a few cascading stems of the white variety of *Euphorbia fulgens*, and one or two stems of longiflorum lilies will give a lightness and warmth to the wedding day.

## RECEPTION FLOWERS

Whether or not the reception is to be held in a house or marquee, it is a good idea to follow the colour scheme through from the church, perhaps using a slightly stronger tone of the colours already used. Incidentally, I have just thought that you cannot really have different strengths of white, can you!

Ideally it is always a good plan to have an important group at the entrance to the house or marquee so that not only is it a welcome, but something for your guests to enjoy whilst they are waiting to be received. The next most important position is by the bridal party, and the third, next to the cake; these are all good focal points. In general, I think that at weddings the whole effect of the flowers, especially if similar in colour to the flowers carried by the bride and bridesmaids, or picked from the colour of their dresses, is most pleasing. If followed through with clever arranging, and if a certain amount of uniformity is attained, it will give a feeling of pleasure on the day.

House flowers I have described in a previous chapter, so there is not much to add except to say you can really let yourself go. If you have a space for a pedestal, this is when you can use it to good advantage as your flowers can then be seen above the guests' heads.

## MARQUEES

These can be awe-inspiring when first encountered, and you get a feeling of despair as you think how can you possibly decorate it to advantage without the use of Kew Gardens? First, just think of it as an extended room, and secondly think of it full of people sitting and standing. Then consider the cake table which is ideal for making a feature group, and so much nicer if it is kept separate from the buffet. Usually, no matter how efficient the caterers are at keeping the buffet free from used glasses and plates, when the time comes to cut the cake it is so much better to be able to turn to a complete setting of its own. So view the marquee with the knowledge of these points in your mind, and plan where the flowers will be seen to best advantage.

First, one's eyes immediately go to the poles which are inevitably there to hold up the tent! They are marvellous objects on which to make some really bold displays. Take three blocks of oasis and tie 2·5 cm/1 in mesh wire netting round each one; place them three quarters of the way up each pole, hanging them on 7·5 cm/3 in nails which you have previously knocked in, and you are then ready to create a cascade of flowers. To carry through the theme, make two trees of flowers for the buffet. These are easily constructed from cut-down broomsticks, fixed on to a square base of 2·5 cm/1 in thick board and topped with a block of oasis covered with wire netting. Place half a block on the base, and away you go to create a smaller version of your poles. I prefer to utilise the poles instead of pedestals which I think look out of place and usually, with the floor not being firm and level, are difficult to keep steady. Stone pedestals and stone urns look particularly fine if filled with a collection of flowering plants or a cascade of rambler roses, especially in the summer. Another idea to conserve flowers is to make square forms of light battening painted white and fixed over white plastic clematis wire. Tie a block of oasis to the back, and create a bunch of flowers rather like a Redouté flower print, using the cut of stems to resemble real ones; and, of course, they can be tied with a classic-type ribbon bow.

## CHRISTENING FLOWERS

These naturally focus round the font – not the easiest of church fittings to decorate. A massed circle, or horseshoe shape, of spring flowers (leaving a space for the vicar to get through) is simple, or a cascade of *Clematis montana* would look lovely for a small girl. Sometimes churches have metal containers which look effective if arranged with small flowers, primroses and violets perhaps, with trails of ivy breaking the line. Or you can make a ring of crushed wire netting with oasis for a

The beautiful Wiltshire home of Captain and Mrs Frederick Barker made an elegant setting for this vase of late autumn flowers gleaned from the garden mixed with added flowers bought from Covent Garden in early November. The foliage were sprays of cotoneaster, eucalyptus, cineraria with an orange-leafed codiaeum as a central feature to give depth and colour. The main blooms were of a salmon anthurium with a surround of *Lilium* 'Golden Clarion'. *Polianthes tuberosa* gave a heady summer perfume, and sprays of orange euphorbia with *Lilium* 'Enchantment' and gerberas carried the apricot colouring through, and the *Lilium auratum* with the cream of the tuberose gave a feeling of lightness. The flowers were arranged in a black antique lead urn with an enamel bowl painted black as a lining; the flowers were held firm by 3·8 cm/1½ in mesh wire netting.

59

filling, placed on a ring of waterproof material into which small flowers can be pushed. If the font is not suitable for garlanding with flowers, try using a small pedestal near the font with a simple arrangement placed on it.

Flowers which can be used include: apple blossom, primroses with moss and trails of ivy, mixed garden pinks with grey foliage, small pompon type dahlias, *Godetia* 'Sybil Sherwood' would be an inexpensive flower for a girl's summer christening. Try small white daisies, the type which grow on inaccessible railway banks, but which are so pretty with small grasses; or, instead, use single white chrysanthemums, 'Bonnie Jean' for white and 'Apricot Springtime' for pink.

## EASTER FLOWERS

The trouble with this festival is its fluctuation of date. The earliest we can have Easter is late March, and the latest is mid-April; so one year you can have masses of flowers, and the next you can be hard put to find the first daffodil.

Yellow and white are, I think, the Easter colours, with cascades of catkins (alder, aspen, hazelnut), branches of *Mahonia bealei*, forsythia, *Cornus mas*, wild white cherry, arum lilies, the Easter lily, *Lilium longiflorum*, crown imperial, *Fritillaria imperialis*, a favourite of the old Dutch painters. One of the legends (of which there are many) concerning this last is that it was the only flower which would not bow its head as Jesus passed to Calvary, so forever after it has bowed its head with unshed tears which are represented by the nectaries. Lilac is mainly found in florists' shops and comes from Holland where it is forced under glass. Wild flowers are in abundance, and are so pretty for the gardens in the church around a model of the crucifix. Blue and white periwinkle, sweet violets (*Viola odorata*), primroses, wood anemones or windflowers, celandines, cowslips, etc, are handy for children to gather and from these they can make their own uninhibited arrangements which are a delight.

One of the most effective Easter displays I have seen was a cross, all of primroses, hanging over the church door. This is easily done on a metal frame covered with moss; then pin on the bunches of primroses, and do include some leaves as this will give a natural look to it.

60

Arum lilies are sometimes a must in some churches, and they are very difficult to arrange because of their thick stems. As they are mainly used on the altar, and as, by tradition, altar vases are usually narrow at their necks, this is an added problem. It is easily overcome by reading my notes on the wiring of vases (Altar Flowers, above). Having done this, place three metal tubes fan-shaped, then start by placing the blooms into the wire netting and tubes, keeping to a fairly formal shape which suits them. Do try and get some leaves to use at the base of the stems. To get a nice curve on the lily, gently run your thumb along the stem of the flower, gently squeezing and bending it at the same time. Unfortunately this works only for a certain length of time after arranging them. Later they all straighten up again, so to have perfection you will just have to bend them again whilst they are still in the vase.

*Lilium longiflorum* or Easter lily, is a much easier one to use as it has a thinner stem and a graceful bloom.

A vase all of forsythia with 2–3 sprays of *Mahonia bealei*, and for the centre several bunches of daffodils, looks very effective. Try using two to three tubes in the arrangement and place a whole bunch of daffodils in a tube; it gives a pleasing look rather than having several daffodils spread over the whole vase; try the same thing with tulips.

Simplicity is a happy note with spring flowers, especially at Easter time. Window sills are a favourite position, and here you could use an oblong cake tin, arranged with catkins, curving branches of weeping willow, and one or two pots of daffodils, with handfuls of moss taken from banks to hide the container and the pots of daffodils.

When arranging a bowl of daffodils, do place them in at all angles so that they retain their natural look. Place several in at a time through the wire netting using the yellow-flowered ivy which is mainly found climbing up trees and known as bunch ivy or *Hedera helix*. If you want to arrange them in oasis break it up first in the bowl as the stems being so soft will only break on the hard block. Or poke a hole with a stick, then push your flowers into it. Small pieces of bun moss or cushion moss are useful for hiding the wire netting.

Another branch type flower usually found around Easter

This simple Christmas arrangement is a favourite with children. It is very easily made as described in the chapter on Christmas decorations. You can make it into a large display by placing it on an old meat dish covered with moss and creating a little garden of winter flowers surrounding it, such as winter jasmin, *Iris unguicularis (I. stylosa)*, Christmas roses, *Helleborus niger*.

This small mixed summer arrangement shown here was the hall of my home in Hertfordshire. It is a combination of white, pale pink and cream flowers. The silver leaves of caladium were the feature of this vase, and before placing them in the arrangement I had dipped the ends of their stems in boiling water to seal them so that they would not droop. The flowers used were *Lilium* 'Silver Queen', *Lilium regale*, white antirrhinum with a pale pink rhododendron and a shocking pink azalea.

time is the sweet-smelling hamamelis or witch hazel; it is so pretty with one or two branches of an evergreen at its base.

## WHITSUN FLOWERS
Whitsun usually calls for red and white flowers. To avoid getting a too-sudden change of colours, try using some silver grey foliage as a background; this will have a softening effect.

## HARVEST FLOWERS
There is an old saying 'September blows soft till the fruit's in the loft'. Apart from the produce from local gardens, allotments and suchlike, it is seasonal to have a vase in the church of all the fruits and berries which can be gathered in hedgerows and which nature provides for us in abundance. Rowan berries, the mountain ash (*Sorbus aucuparia*), viburnum or guelder rose, with red berries, sprays of blackberries, sweet chestnuts, hips, haws, all these placed together in a copper coal scuttle or bowl with heads and sprays of pale green *Hydrangea quercifolia*, and *Hydrangea paniculata* with its pointed cream to pinky heads, with a few bunches of purple grapes and a trail or two of the passion flower, would provide a true essence of the harvest spirit.

Also at this time there are some beautiful berried shrubs such as the *Cotoneaster* genus. Take a few sprays of the fan-shaped branches of *C. horizontalis*, place it in a vase with the scarlet dahlia 'Love's Dream', and with several heads of *Hydrangea paniculata*, and one or two stems of *Sedum* 'Autumn Joy', and you will have a very splendid harvest vase.

When arranging the proverbial marrow, pumpkin and endless apples, try grouping them with trails of clematis travellers' joy, (old man's beard,) sprays of sweet chestnut and berries in large baskets or even wooden boxes; or group them under pedestal arrangements where trails of passion flowers can cascade on to them. One of the most attractive groupings of fruits and vegetables I have seen was of golden pumpkins, custard marrows with sprays of coppery vine leaves, and purple grapes trailing over them.

When using dahlias and hydrangeas in autumn arrangements, place the ends of the stalks in $1\,\mathrm{cm}/\frac{1}{2}$ in hot water for a few moments; this will help to keep them fresh.

## BOUQUETS

There is a feeling today that it is usual for the bride to carry white flowers, and I personally think that all-white bouquets are the most beautiful. They create a feeling of fragility and softness against the white dress, and if a colour is required the bridesmaids can have bouquets to match or contrast with their dresses. Longiflorum lilies, with their waxy white sheen and pale green centres, would look superb on a mediaeval-style dress, whereas the star-shaped stephanotis blooms would look lovely cascading down a dress of white organza. Round flowers look best in a posy type bouquet, and long flowing blooms look best in a shower type. There are many flowers suitable for both brides and bridesmaids to carry, and as the making of bouquets is a specialised form of floristry I do advocate leaving it to the experts to create a thing of beauty for you.

If you really wish to make a bouquet, forget about the wiring and rather, when you have bought or gathered the flowers you wish to use, put them into a sheaf-like bunch tying them with a ribbon to match the dresses. For younger bridesmaids try using a small basket; line it with moss or a small block of oasis and fill it with small-headed flowers in the colour required.

When suggesting the form of the flower decorations, including the bouquets, I am quite often asked who traditionally pays for them. Nowadays it is usually a joint venture as it is rather too much for one side to foot the bill. But the general idea used to be that the bride's and bridesmaids' flowers were a gift from the bridegroom, and the church flowers were paid for by the bride's family. It is nice to hear of the old traditions even if they are not strictly adhered to these days.

This silver bowl of commercially grown Baccara roses, which can look very stiff and uninteresting if used on their own, was helped considerably by the use of rose foliage trails, such as those of *Rosa rubrifolia* with its purplish sheen on the foliage. This was an asset as it looked so well against the dark red of the rose petals.

# 7 Exhibiting Flowers

## FLOWER SHOWS

One of my very favourite pastimes is to visit the local flower shows wherever I am. Not only to see and wonder at the largest marrows and the longest leeks, but to see the young peoples' arrangements of wild flowers, perhaps in a jam jar or home-made container; I feel you can learn a great deal from them, all being so simple and uncontrived. I will leave the flower club shows to the professionals to write about because they are so specialised these days I would not know where to begin; so here are just a few general thoughts about them.

Let us say you have taken the plunge, or been persuaded to enter for a class set out in a schedule. Now the most important step is to read it thoroughly, and then re-read it. Because even if your vase is the highlight of the show, if it does not conform to the rules laid down, you may well be disqualified. If you are not sure on a point or two, have it explained by a member of the committee; this will avoid a disappointment.

When judging an exhibit I would expect to find that:
1 The exhibitor has read the rules.
2 The arrangement is in proportion to the space and correct measurements laid down.
3 It has good design.
4 It has good harmony.
5 That the flowers and foliage are in good condition.
6 The technique is good in its construction, plus its relation to the receptacle.
7 It has originality.

A helpful way to work out the space allotted is to cut out a piece of paper to the size of the alcove, or mark it in pencil on a wall. Have a trial run using the container, accessories, drape fabric, ornaments, etc, so that you can be sure you have chosen the correct equipment. When choosing a container that will fill the space you have been given remember a safe rule is the flowers should be one and a half times the height of the vase. For instance if your total height available was 115 cm/45 in, your vase should be roughly 46 cm/18 in.

Having worked out the space and decided on your vase, drapes, fabrics, figurines, etc, start working out the details of your arrangement, the theme, and the colouring. If it is a Victorian theme which is required, make sure that all the accessories are of the right period and so on.

Always wire your vase the previous day; if using a pin holder, fix it firmly. If a block of oasis is used, give it a good soak for 24 hours.

Pick your foliage and gather or buy your flowers in plenty of time to be able to give them all the right conditioning, eg lilac needs hot water and sugar, delphiniums the same; dahlias and milky stems need sealing at their ends. When choosing foliage go for the more mature leaves as fresh young foliage, no matter how pretty and attractive it is, does tend to wilt. Try and have duplicates of your flowers and foliage so as to be able to replace any that do wilt.

Last of all, give yourself plenty of time, and double-check before you leave home that you have everything you need, including a thermos of coffee to give yourself a reviving drink.


## MINIATURE ARRANGEMENTS

A miniature arrangement might be called the flower arranger's nightmare, but during the past years it has become a must at many a flower club show or WI meeting. The miniature exhibit is usually the one that draws the crowds who marvel at the deftness of the touch of the arranger. The size of miniature arrangements is considered by many flower clubs to be 15 cm/6 in overall, but I have seen many much smaller and I am sure that they must be done by using a magnifying glass. I think 14 cm/5·6 in is a fair size, but I have seen schedules that say 'Not to exceed 7·5 cm/3 in in any dimension, and to be shown on a mirror base' . . . . 'In a small sea shell, in association with a group of doll's furniture', and so on. Clearly it must be left for the show authorities to stipulate the size.

A miniature arrangement may develop from seeing an interesting container, or perhaps you have seen it on a flower show schedule which attracts you to enter. Miniature arrangements are really a large vase done on a small scale, and the principles which govern the larger arrangement apply in exactly the same way to the small one: it must have balance, design and harmony. Please do not overcrowd your tiny vase; each flower must show its own beauty. Textures play an important part. Dainty flowers go in silver or glass, whilst pottery really needs a coarser type of flower; a small round bowl would need round flowers; a narrow-necked vase would be more suitable for tiny blade-like grasses.

Tweezers with a small point and nail or sewing scissors are all the tools you really need. You can try using your own fingers, if you are not too ham-fisted like myself; but hands do get in the way, no matter how nimble you are.

A small wooden base to your arrangement gives a finished look to it, or a small round pocket mirror, or try looking in a Chinese handicraft shop for little oriental-type bases. A piece of silk or a delicate lace handkerchief as an accessory just gives the finishing touch; but remember to choose the right colour and texture to add to the harmony. Tiny figurines can also be used and will add height and, at the same time, emphasise the smallness of the arrangement. On the other hand, another way round is to use a small figure to give the same effect in reverse: shells picked up on the beach with a small piece of driftwood, a silver thimble with a lace hand-kerchief, an eggshell with a small china bird, to name but a few ideas. Do remember a small vase with full-size blooms cut down is not a substitute for a thimble with tiny Cecile Brunner roses, together with tiny sprigs of gypsophila and small sprays of the grey sedum.

By walking along country roads you will see an abundance of suitable materials, and this would be a chance for an early introduction for children to take an interest in flowers and the arranging of them. You will find grasses, buttercups, celandines, cow parsley flowers, berries, wild dog roses with their tiny buds, all suitable for your arrangements.

This mantlepiece arrangement in the height of summer was one of a pair. The flowers used were *Lilium regale* and *L.* 'Silver Queen', with *Paeonia* 'Sarah Bernhardt'. The foliage was stripped lime branches with arching stems of *Escallonia* 'Apple Blossom'. When arranging flowers on a mantlepiece it is vitally important to make sure it is sitting comfortably on the mantle shelf or instead you will have a floor arrangement! Sit your flowers well back in the vase when starting. If your container is too light, weight the vase by either placing stones in it or, if there is room, tie a brick on to the back of the wire netting holding the flowers. Also make sure that you have some sweeping trails of foliage to fall gracefully over the edge of the vase so that it actually incorporates the mantlepiece into the arrangement.

# 8 Dried Flowers

## DRIED ARRANGEMENTS:
## ARTIFICIAL FLOWERS

Once you have become interested in the arrangement of dried flowers the possibilities are endless. All you need is a perceptive eye as you go searching for dried materials: the hedgerows and fields are full of lovely grasses, seed pods, and the white, scaly grey fungi which you can find on silver birch trees.

One of the easiest of the wild plants to dry and usually available in most parts of the country, is travellers' joy, also known as old man's beard. Pick it before the seed pods have become fluffy; it takes glycerine and water marvellously. (I put one part glycerine to two parts hot water.) I think it is one of the prettiest of wild flowers when dried. I remember seeing two tall alabaster urns arranged just with old man's beard; all the leaves had been stripped off and only the cascading seed heads remained. In fact these, in the first place, had been cut and placed in water, and they just dried themselves; what could be easier?

Dried flowers are an absolute blessing in the months when flowers are at a premium; on a special occasion you can always add the odd stem of fresh flowers. I remember doing this to a friend's vase. It consisted of sprays of bracken, allium heads, corn, achillea, angelica heads, and branches covered with lichen. For a special evening in early June I just added some stems of a yellow lily; the pale yellow blended so beautifully with the dull greens and beige of the dried flowers that all her friends thought that the lilies were dried as well! To save the dried flower stems from getting wet I used metal tubes in which to place the flowers, or you could use glass test tubes.

Hydrangeas are other useful flowers to dry, and very easy. Cut the hydrangeas when the flowers have been on the plant for several weeks, and just when the flowers are changing to red and green, strip them of their leaves and place them in 5–7·5 cm/2–3 in of hot water. Leave them in a warm room, and you will find they will dry beautifully.

Bamboo and *Osmunda regalis* dry splendidly if you place them between newspaper under a heavy carpet or weights, and leave them till dry. They take on a beautiful celadon green colour, and with the addition of dry green hydrangea, some seed pods, and some yellow achillea heads, you have the makings of an effective vase.

There are so many specialist books on the art of drying flowers that I will just touch on the simpler ways which I find effective.

## PRESSING

This is marvellous for all plants that have a natural habitually flat growth, eg *Osmunda regalis* which I have already mentioned, bamboo, bracken, beech, crocosmia, montbretia, sweet chestnut, to name but a few. Hellebore leaves take on the same lovely celadon green as osmunda and bamboo; the crocosmia, if picked when just turning brown, retains this colour. When you have pressed these leaves they are very brittle. To strengthen them, take thin canes and attach them to the main stem, or obtain some florist's wires and wire the leaves. Remember that all these are very flat-looking, so get some hydrangeas to give a round look and depth to your arrangement. Or look around in a flower shop or plant centre for the unusual seed pods from abroad such as wood roses from America (*Ipomoea tuberosa*), lotus pods and many others.

## GLYCERINE TREATMENT

This is a composition of glycerine, usually obtainable from a chemist, and hot water – one part glycerine to two parts hot water. Beech is splendid and reacts well, but a lot is trial and error. Take branches of hips, eucalyptus, *Magnolia grandiflora*, old man's beard. After splitting and hammering the

72

stems, place them in a container so that at least 15 cm/6 in extends into the solution. As the branches take it up, the leaves turn golden, brown or bronze, the colour depending on the type of foliage. Be sure you make a good quantity of the solution if you have a lot of foliage as some branches take up more than others. Re-cut the stems once a week, 1–2·5 cm/½–1 in each time, as this will accelerate the process–it takes about two to three weeks–and remove when you obtain the colour you require. One advantage about glycerined foliage is that it can be used with fresh flowers as the water will not harm treated stems. If you have time and the inclination, do experiment as this could be fun and most interesting; you might even find a new subject that will intrigue your friends.

## SKELETONISING

This is a very specialised process, and I would advise trying to buy some leaves from either a florist who gets them from abroad, or perhaps a friend who has mastered the art. It is, in fact, the process of dissolving the green matter and leaving just the ribs of the leaf. Magnolias and rhododendrons are the best subjects. The magnolia looks lovely bound on to bare branches, slightly gilted and glittered, and used for Christmas decorations. I have two magnolia leaves at my home which have birds painted on them; they may be years old, and were obviously done by a person with a very delicate touch.

## POT POURRI

This can be made by picking fragrant flowers and foliage in the morning before the dew evaporates. Select only the most perfect materials. Split all the blossoms, pull the leaves from the stems and spread them thinly over newspapers to dry. Lay the newspapers on a rack so that the air can circulate above and below. While the moisture is being absorbed, you will find the newspapers become damp, so change them; dry the flowers in an airy, dry room. When dry, they should have the texture of cornflakes. These can then be stored in tightly covered jars or tins. Then use any recipe to your liking; you can find them in various books on dried flowers. Orris root is one of the ingredients.

Flowers and foliage suitable for pot pourri include: laven-

der, love-in-the-mist, verbena, anaphalis, roses and mari-
golds.

**Recipe for Pot Pourri** 4 oz orris root, 3 oz oil of cloves, 2 oz
gum benzoin, 4 oz calamus root, 6 oz angelica root, 10 drops
true oil of cinnamon. 40 drops essence of bergamot, 40 drops
English oil of lavender. 30 drops oil of verbena. Sprinkle some
salt amongst your petals and leave to stand a few days. Then
pour the above mixture over them.

## HANGING FLOWERS TO DRY

This is one of the easiest methods of drying flowers, and the
one you can have most fun with as you can experiment as you
go along. Pick the flowers when nearly fully out; experience
alone will guide you. Delphiniums, acanthus, moluccella,
should have their flowers out right to their tips. Everlasting
flowers like anaphalis, helichrysum and statice can be picked
in the advanced bud form. Strip all foliage from the flowers and
tie them in small bunches in a warm airy room: moluccella,
bells of Ireland, verbascums, artichokes, hollyhocks, alchemilla, grasses, delphiniums ('Blue Bee' variety does very well),
and hydrangeas. But do remember not to place them too close
together or they will shatter when pulling them apart. Tie the
stems tightly as they will shrink and are liable to fall down.
Flowers dry better and retain their colour if dried quickly; the
boiler room is ideal if there is plenty of air circulating. Some
flowers will need the help of a wire or two. Take some florist's
wires the right thickness for their stems, and for the
helichysums or zinnias, push it through the flower's head.

## ARRANGING DRIED FLOWERS

As they need no water you can use a variety of containers
which would usually not be suitable for fresh flowers. Driftwood is fun to collect and looks well with drieds. Baskets and
alabaster urns sometimes come with a tiny space, so use some
oasis fix and a ball of wire netting which will be sufficient to
hold the dried flowers. These will be light in weight so, with all
containers, fill the vase with dry silver sand or stones before
putting in your wire netting or dry oasis with which to hold the
flowers, and then to hide any wire netting showing after
finishing your vase, try finding some grey lichen, the sort

74

reindeer eat; it can be found where heather grows. Use it damp, and it takes on a lovely pearl grey colour when dry; or use broken hydrangea heads. Another idea to use up flower heads and seed pods is to make a cone of oasis, cover it with 2·5 cm/1 in wire netting and, using a small stick to make a hole, stick in the materials making the shape of a pyramid. At Christmas time, if you get bored with it, you can always spray it with one of the aerosol paint sprays. Gold and silver is a good mixture, and by adding a few scarlet ribbons, it would

A symphony of white flowers in a table centre for a wedding breakfast. When using all one colour in an arrangement it is advisable to employ as many shapes and textures as possible. Here I used sweet peas, carnations, roses and gerberas, but very little foliage. To create lightness I hid the mechanics, ie wire netting, with some large leaves of the house plant dieffenbachia and a few fronds of a pale green fern. Always remember to keep your flowers low so that the guests can see over them.

take pride of place on a table. Branches will give form and line to your arrangement, so look out for gnarled wisteria branches, magnolia, willow, *Salix matsudana* 'Tortuosa', *Corylus contorta* and twisted hazel.

## FLOWERS, LEAVES AND SEED PODS SUITABLE FOR DRYING

Acanthus (F)
Alchemilla (F)
Alliums (F)
Anaphalis (F)
Astrantia (F)
Atriplex (S)
Bamboo (L)
Beech (L)
*Briza Maxima* (Quaking Grass) (S)
Clematis (Old Man's Beard) (L & F)
Delphinium 'Blue Bee' (F)
Echinops (F)
Eryngium (F)
Eucalyptus (L)
Evening Primrose (S)
Gypsophila (F)
Helichrysums (F)
Hollyhocks (F)
Hydrangea (F)
*Magnolia grandiflora* (L)
Moluccella (S)
*Osmunda regalis* (L)
Pampas Grass (F)
Physalis (Chinese Lantern) (F)
*Stachys lanata* (F)
Statice (F)
Verbascum (F)
Zinnias (F)

F = Flowers; L = Leaves; S = Seed pods
This collection will give you a good choice of material.

# 9 Treatment of Flowers

I agree with the sentiments of a flower arranger who, on hearing I was to write a book, beseeched me to include a chapter on flowers and their different treatment. I quote from her letter: 'Nothing is more irritating than to spend so much time picking flowers, crushing stems, putting into deep water for hours, etc, etc, and then the next day they have flopped regardless.' She certainly has all my commiserations as it also at times happens to me. I have mentioned in most of the chapters of this book, where applicable, how to condition flowers and foliage. In this chapter I am going to list a few plants which I feel would be useful in the garden, and after each one are the methods of conditioning them for using in arrangements. But if you find your own pet ways work – aspirin, lemonade, etc – do carry on with them. There is always an exception to the rule, and I often find on the odd occasion that it is the bowl I have literally thrown together at the last moment without any special conditioning, which lasts best.

My own way is to fill my vase or container with hot water, and to split all stems that need splitting. I find that the flowers that need hot water treatment love it, those which dislike it just have to put up with it, and nine times out of ten, it works.

### *Acanthus* (Bear's Breeches)
A strikingly handsome plant with shining, dark green leaves which in winter can be used very successfully if treated with a solution of glycerine and water. It has tall, noble spikes of mauve and white flowers which last well in water after first dipping their ends in boiling water. Hang them up to dry them off for winter decoration.

Here is my favourite container; a silver Victorian basket filled with an interesting collection of early summer flowers in shades of mauve and pale pink. To show off the two tulips, *Tulipa viridiflora* I used heads of lilac with pale pink tulips, the shocking pink gerbera with sprays of the pink 'Doris'. The foliage was elephant grey, using *Senecio greyii*, seed pods of *Mahonia bealei* together with sprays of *Stachys lanata* and the blue-grey leaves of hosta.

### *Achillea* (**Milfoil or Yarrow**)
A very useful flat-headed flower of pale yellow is 'Moonshine' or there is a deeper yellow with feathery grey foliage called 'Coronation Gold'. This lasts well in water and dries beautifully if hung up. It is marvellous for autumn arrangements.

### *Alchemilla mollis* (**Lady's Mantle**)
This green feathery flower is a must for a flower arranger. It is so easy to grow from seed and will seed itself, once established, all over the garden; but it can be increased also by division. It likes a damp, moist, shady position which helps it to keep its colour, but it will also grow in full sun. It will dry quite well keeping its colour, and needs no special treatment except warm water if soft.

### *Alstroemeria*
The *A. ligtu* hybrids are most attractive but are not entirely hardy. Most people know only of the orange herbaceous plant, but do try a few of these from seed. They are a little ungainly in growth, so grow them in a spare piece of ground where they can romp away. They last well in water, and have very good seed pods.

### *Amaranthus* (**Love Lies Bleeding**)
Apart from the red one, the greenish-white form *A. caudatus* 'Viridis' with its green tails gives a good cascade effect in an arrangement. It is a half-hardy annual which likes being fed. Remove all the leaves, hammer the stems, and place in hot water. Every spring it produces marvellous branches of blue-grey foliage. It takes glycerine and water mixture very well, and when preserved in this way it takes on a lovely reddish hue.

### *Angelica*
This is a hardy perennial easily grown from seed. It has enormous green flower heads and looks best in white arrangements or in a foliage group. Place the ends of the stem in boiling water first; it dries well if hung up.

### *Artemisia nutans*
A lovely feathery-grey foliage plant. It grows well on poorish light soil in full sun. Place ends of stems in hot water; it is

very pretty with pale pink or blue flowers. *A. lactiflora* is taller with creamy-white, lacy, decorative plumes 1·4 m/ 54 in high. It likes moisture and partial shade. Hammer the stems and place in hot water; when in seed it dries well if hung up.

### *Arum italicum* 'Marmoratum'

This is used chiefly because it has a very distinct marbled leaf. It appears first in late autumn and is lovely used with small spring flowers. In the late summer it produces magnificent stems of red, fleshy berries.

Condition by placing in warm water.

### *Astrantia maxima*

A pinkish white flower, it is very pretty with summer flowers. It has a peculiar smell which is unpleasant in a small room. Place it in warm water.

### *Atriplex hortensis*

This purple flowering spinach is splendid for using in a large arrangement. It produces tall spikes of leaves and flowers 1·2–1·5 m/4–5 ft long.

Condition by removing base leaves and hammer ends of stems, then place in 5–7·5 cm/2–3 in of boiling water.

### *Ballota*

This is a late spring woolly flowering plant which has whorls of green flowers. It is best when the leaves are removed, and for conditioning, place the stems in boiling water.

### *Bergenia (Megasea; Pig Squeak)*

*B. delavayi* has purple flowers, green oval leaves in spring, crimson in winter. It is a marvellous plant for use all the year round. Sometimes in early autumn hidden leaves take on a pale yellow and coral colouring. It is very effective when mixed with roses or dahlias; the green leaves look marvellous in green arrangements of foliage. Soak leaves in cold water overnight before arranging.

### *Bocconia* or *Macleaya*

A tall feathery hardy perennial. The variety 'Coral Plume' has deep buff-coloured flowers suitable for tall arrangements. Pick them only when the last flowers are showing. Boil the stems before arranging; leave stems on the plant for dried arrangements.

### *Caladium* (Angel's Wings)
This is a stove house perennial plant. It has beautiful heart-shaped leaves of green and white or various shades of pink. Either use the whole plant in an arrangement, or use the cut leaves after dipping the stems in boiling water.

### *Camellia japonica*
One of our best evergreen shrubs. It is marvellous for winter decoration if your plant is large enough to pick from. Or use the flowers by floating them in a bowl. Condition these by hammering stems and placing them in warm water.

### *Cedrus atlantica glauca*
This is the blue pine with lovely cones, so pretty to use at Christmas time with variegated holly and pale grey eucalyptus foliage. It lasts well in water, and is very useful for making evergreen garlands.

### *Chimonanthus* (Winter Sweet)
This strongly scented winter flowering shrub, which flowers on leafless branches, is a favourite of mine. One stem will scent the whole room when picked. It originally came from China, and bundles of the twigs were often placed in linen cupboards so that the linen picked up their fragrance.
    Condition by hammering stems and placing in warm water.

### *Choisya ternata* (Mock Orange Bush)
Half-hardy evergreen shrub with sweet-smelling white flowers, useful for its foliage and when it is in flower. Hammer the stems and place in warm water.

### *Clematis montana*
One of the easiest to grow, and so effective trailing from tall groups; or use on a font with apple blossom. Hammer stems

and put in hot water. The wild *Clematis vitalba* is a great joy to use in all its forms, flowering and seeding. You can dry old man's beard before it gets too fluffy in a solution of glycerine and water.

### Cobaea scandens
A bell-shaped flowering climbing plant, it starts off cream and gradually shades to a soft lilac hue. There is a green variety too, half-hardy and easily grown from seed. It has been known to over-winter in a sheltered spot.

### Cotoneaster
This is a valuable evergreen or deciduous shrub, particularly good for its autumn-fruiting orange to scarlet berries. It always seems to do well in the centre of motorways! Hammer stems and spray berries with a leaf shine to keep.

### Crocosmia (Montbretia)
Hardy perennial with orange flowers in arching sprays with gladioli-like leaves which dry to a pale yellow colour if placed under a carpet or between blotting paper.

### Cynara scolymus or C. cardunculus Artichoke (Globe)
This has a beautifully cut silver grey leaf and a bulbous flower head which you can eat! – or place it in a vase. It can be grown easily from seed and is very useful indeed. Place ends of stems in boiling water, flower stems as well as leaves. The young leaves are notorious for wilting, so wait till they are older before picking. The flowers will dry very well if hung up.

### Dahlia
A must for flower arrangers. It comes in a variety of colours, shapes and sizes from miniature to pompon, from the small decorative varieties to giant flowering cactus.

Conditioning: Cut the flowers just after they have fully opened. Take care to remove all leaves which will be below water level. Place in hand hot water or in 5–7·5 cm/2–3 in of boiling water; both methods work.

82

The use here of pale green leaves together with tulips enhanced the heads of azalea. *Tulipa viridiflora* 'Artist' with its rose-pink petals and green stripes, were a perfect foil to the narcissus and green seed pods of the hellebore. Sprays of the green bells of tellima gave lightness together with the pale green and yellow leaves of *Hosta fortunei*. To pick up the rose shading of the 'Artist' tulip I used a spray of a pink form of *Clematis montana*. As with all early spring flowers I conditioned them by arranging them in warm water.

### Delphinium

Hardy herbaceous perennial. Blue, white and the variety called 'Blue Bee' are all very useful for larger arrangements; they like hot water with sugar added. 'Blue Bee' variety dries particularly well if hung up in a warm room.

### Dianthus (Carnation)

A large family of greenhouse carnations, border pinks and alpine varieties. The two we usually come across and use often are the greenhouse carnations and border pink 'Doris'. These are some of our most lasting cut flowers and remain fresh for up to ten days or more.

Conditioning: The stems have hard nodes which makes it difficult for water to pass through, so cut stems at an angle. Place in warm water overnight having removed a little foliage from the base. Incidentally, the leaves do not decay quickly in water and, if left on, help the flower to absorb more water.

### Digitalis (Foxglove)

Hardy biennial, a very pretty and useful flower for early summer groups. Some seed merchants stock the lovely hybrids 'Excelsior' which have flowers all round the stem. Suttons used to have the seeds for the lovely apricot variety which unfortunately they no longer stock. So shop around for seed as it's a must in a garden. Place ends of stems in hot water.

### Elaeagnus

This is a lovely group of evergreen shrubs; all varieties are a delight for winter use, especially *E. pungens* 'Maculata' which is liberally splashed with deep golden-yellow with green at edges, and a very pretty grey one with arching sprays of silver leaves is *E. macrophylla*. They last well in water which needs changing quite often as they are rather apt to make the water smell after a time, use a few drops of bleach in the water to help with this problem.

### Enkianthus

An early-flowering summer shrub which likes peaty soil. Flowers are open bell-shaped in small pendulous clusters, creamy-white at the base, purplish-pink nearer tips, good for autumn colour. Hammer stems and put in warm water.

## *Eryngium*
Teasel-like metallic blue flowers. The best species is *E. giganteum*, silvery blue, sometimes known as 'Miss Willmott's Ghost'. It is excellent for drying.

## *Eucalyptus*
Australia's gracious gift to the world. There are several hardy species worth growing; the most popular, *E. gunnii*, grows easily from seed. If growth is cut down every spring, it will retain its young foliage which is a paler shade of grey.

## *Euphorbia pulcherrima* (Poinsettia)
A tender greenhouse plant, but now the House of Rochford has produced a long-lasting pot variety in pink, white and red. Do not cut the stems as they bleed, but wash the roots of soil and use the whole plant.

## *Euphorbia* (Spurge)
This is a good hardy herbaceous genus and is marvellous for the flower arranger. All have milky stems, so either place ends in 2·5cm/1in hot water or burn the ends. *E. wulfenii* is very stately and has lovely lacy spikes of yellow flowers; *E. polychroma* is short-stemmed but has lovely bracts of bright yellow flowers; *E. griffithii* 'Fireglow' has orange and red bracts.

## *Forsythia*
If the birds do not eat all the flowers, which they love, it is a marvellous shrub for using with spring flowers, or a very happy combination is of branches of forsythia with stems of *Mahonia bealei*. It can be easily forced by bringing it into a cool dark room; spraying the wood with water from time to time helps it to flower.

Condition by cutting just below or through a node as stems are hollow in between. Place in cold water.

This galaxy of early summer flowers consisted of pale blue delphiniums, *Lilium* 'Rubrum', *L.* 'Destiny' and *L. regale*, yellow antirrhinum, purple allium heads with late pink rhododendron. Foliage used was Solomon's seal, copper beech and *Rosa rubrifolia*. It was arranged in a pink marble *tazza* to match the marble background.

**Forcing Flowering Shrubs**

Here seems an opportune time to mention the forcing of flowering shrubs. The best results are gained when the buds of flowering shrubs begin to swell in late winter and early spring. If you cut too soon the buds are liable to drop. A good guide of when to pick the branches of a shrub to force is to consider its normal flowering time and cut 6–8 weeks ahead. As I write – during the first week of February – I have myself just cut some flowering cherry. You can cut earlier, but the flowers will not be as good.

Hammer the stems and place in cold water in a room with a temperature between 13°–18°C/55°–65°F. Change the water frequently; charcoal can be used to keep the water fresh, but it is not essential. Each time you change the water do re-cut the ends of the stems. Spray with water at least once a week as it has the same effect as the rain; it also helps the buds to develop and open.

Do not place the branches where direct sunlight will fall on them as this will have the effect of drying the buds and causing them to fall off. A cool greenhouse is an ideal place or a sun room. As the buds open, move them into a brighter light to intensify the colour; if left in semi-shade you will get pale flowers. Incidentally, the 'Hizakura' cherry is far nicer forced in shade as its flowers are of palest pink with a tissue paper texture, quite exquisite with its pale green leaves.

If you wish to hurry up the forcing process, you can place the branches in hot, nearly boiling water once a day. If too far advanced for the desired time, place back again in a cool, shady place until you want to use them.

*Fritillaria imperialis* **(Crown Imperial)**

This is an orange or yellow flowering bulbous flower which has rather an unpleasant smell.

Conditioning: no special treatment is required – the stems are rather apt to split and curl up at the ends so these can be tied with string. Flowers end of March and April.

*Garrya elliptica*

An evergreen shrub with the male plant bearing beautiful

grey-green catkins in January/February. The female plant has grey-green seed pods resembling bunches of grapes turning to purple when ripe. The birds are very fond of them, so get there before they do. The male plant is very useful for forcing. Conditioning: Hammer stems and put in warm water.

### Hamamelis (Witch Hazel)
Deciduous shrub flowering late January–several varieties available–very sweet smelling–clusters of yellow flowers. One branch in a room will fill it with its sweet scent. Conditioning: hammer stems and put in warm water.

### Hosta (Funkia)
These are absolutely marvellous for the flower arranger, and very easy to grow in a moist spot; in fact I have seen them growing well in dry places as well. They range in colour from dark green through to lime green, yellow and variegated. Conditioning: do not pick them too young, and submerge in water for several hours before using.

### Hydrangea
These are good garden plants giving you weeks of colour, and are excellent for cutting. The lace-cap varieties are very attractive, and also the painted, creamy-pink flower of *H. paniculata*. The green-white *H. arborescens* 'Grandiflora' is also very useful to the flower arranger.

Conditioning: place ends of stems in boiling water, then submerge heads and stems in water for an hour or two. When you have them arranged in a vase it helps if you spray when you can with a fine spray of water.

### Lunaria (Honesty)
Besides the well-known variety with its purple flowers and seed pods used in winter dried groups, commonly called 'Silver Pennies', there is a lovely variegated one which is almost cream with pale lilac flowers. Conditioning: place ends of stems in hot water and then give a long drink of water.

### Lysichiton (Skunk Cabbage)
This is my favourite bog plant with spathes of yellow. They

88

also have marvellous seed heads which look very good in foliage arrangements. Conditioning: no special treatment, but if the flowers flag, place ends of stems in hot water.

### *Mahonia bealei*
This has lovely sprays of yellow flowers, with a perfume similar to lily-of-the valley, flowering in winter. Leaves turn a beautiful colour in the autumn. The berries are blue with a grey bloom – very pretty in small arrangements. Conditioning: hammer stems and place in warm water.

### *Moluccella* (bells of Ireland)
This flower is insignificant, but it is surrounded by a large cup-shaped, pale green calyx. It is easy to grow from seed, and dries beautifully. To use, remove all leaves and place stems in warm water.

### *Nerine*
This is a greenhouse bulb, but the species *N. bowdenii* grows very well out of doors in a sheltered position, and has pink lily-like flowers in early autumn. *N. sarniensis* needs to be grown indoors and has vermilion-coloured flowers. Both species are excellent for flower arrangers and last well. Conditioning: cut the ends and give them a long drink in warm water.

### *Nicotiana* (Tobacco Flower)
'Daylight' which stays open all day and 'Lime Green' are two varieties worth growing. Conditioning: remove bottom leaves and place in warm water.

### *Onopordum*
A beautiful grey thistle which can be used as a whole branch, or the leaves can be used separately. Conditioning: place ends of leaves and stems in boiling water. Be careful of the thorns which can be very painful.

### *Ornithogalum nutans*
With greenish-grey star-like flowers, these are lovely when used in green arrangements; they flower in spring. *O. thyrsoides*

is the chincherinchee which grows in winter in South Africa and in June with us. They are far more useful in the winter as they last for about seven weeks in water. They are very attractive grown as pot plants. Conditioning: the imported ones from South Africa need the waxed ends cut off and the stems placed in warm water; the same treatment can be applied to the English variety.

### *Papaver orientale*
This is a large greyish-pink flower with purple-black blotches at the base; it is lovely for a grey arrangement. Conditioning: burn ends of stems or place in boiling water.

### *Parrotia*
A lovely shrub for autumn colouring, turning brilliant orange-red in October. Conditioning: split ends of stems and place in warm water. The foliage can be sprayed with leaf shine as it helps it to last that much longer.

### *Philadelphus*
This is a lovely white flowering shrub which smells strongly of orange; it is usually known as mock orange and often wrongly as syringa. It lasts well in water if the leaves are removed first. Conditioning: split or hammer ends and place in hot water. Never leave it out of water once it has drunk, and always pick it when it is nearly fully out.

### *Polygonatum multiflorum* (Solomon's Seal)
This is a flower arranger's must. It has arching branches with white pendulous flowers. It grows in most places, and Lanning Roper told me once that to get it to grow you should plant lily-of-the-valley with it. After the flowers have finished, it sometimes produces green seeds.
Conditioning: cut when flowers are nearly out to the tip, and place in warm water.

### *Prunus* (Flowering Cherry)
These are deciduous trees grown for their profusely-borne pink, white or cream flowers, and also for their brilliant autumn colouring of foliage. *P. subhirtella* 'Autumnalis' is

A tall pedestal arrangement was needed in this ballroom so as to be out of the reach of the dancers. The flowers were arranged in a large china bowl painted black to match the pedestal, the bowl being the type used in the old days for bedrooms. The flowers were apricot foxgloves, pink double stocks, pink antirrhinums, *Lilium* 'Rubrum' with foliage of stripped lime, philadelphus, Solomon's seal with trails of passiflora. Wire netting was used to hold the flowers in the bowl, and metal tubes on sticks helped to extend the length of the shorter flower stems.

valuable for its winter flowering, and is so pretty with delicate flowers of *Iris unguicularis* which can be picked in bud. Conditioning: hammer ends of stems and place in warm water. To force other varieties place in a warm room from January onwards and spray stems frequently. *P.* 'Kanzan' also known as *P.* 'Sekiyama' is probably the best for forcing. *P. triloba* is much smaller shrub species which is also excellent for forcing.

### *Pyracantha coccinea* (Firethorn)
A useful evergreen shrub which has lovely berries in the autumn, but it is also very spiteful as it has long thorns. A pretty species which has a more droopy habit and produces lovely, long, trailing branches clustered with golden/yellow or reddish/orange berries, is *P. rogersiana*. Conditioning: hammer stems and place in deep water. Spray berries with leaf shine.

### *Pyrus* (Pear)
*P. salicifolia* 'Pendula' is the silver willow pear which has silver foliage, and is one of our finest silvery-leaved small trees. Conditioning: hammer stems and put in warm water; it lasts well.

### *Rhododendron* (including Azalea)
These are a must for the flower arranger who has a lime-free soil garden. The range of hybrids is enormous so, before buying them, do go to the RHS shows, or to the Savill Gardens near Windsor or Wisley Gardens at Ripley in Surrey, to see and take note of the colours that appeal to you. I planted several dozen plants of rhododendrons and azaleas in the garden of my home in 1957, and today we are cutting freely from them. Conditioning: hammer stems gently or they will break, and place in hot water. It is a good idea to remove the leaves from around the flower of the rhododendron so as to expose the flowers. Some of the smaller varieties are better if all the leaves are removed before arranging them.

### *Ribes* (Flowering Currant)
One of the best shrubs to force for flowering indoors from mid-January. It also makes an excellent garden shrub.

Conditioning: hammer ends of stems and place in deep water. When forcing, spray the branches with water as this keeps the wood moist enabling it to flower better. When forced ribes flowers are always white.

### Rosa (Rose)
This is an enormous family giving untold pleasure from the first rose plucked in June to the last one gathered in November. Everybody has their favourites so I will not enumerate them. The old fashioned roses are very popular with a lovely scent, and they are so pretty in mixed arrangements or just on their own. The floribundas are also a must, such free flowering varieties as 'Apricot Nectar', 'Iceberg', 'Pascali Cream', 'Iced Ginger' (apricot), 'Rosemary'. They have no smell, but have lovely foliage to compensate.

### Rosa rubrifolia
This is a very useful foliage rose having silvery, purplish leaves and later on, clusters of orange hips. Conditioning: after putting the hammered ends in boiling water, give them a long drink.

### Sedum spectabile
The flowers range from rich pink to the rose-salmon of the variety 'Autumn Joy'. They have flat heads borne on glaucous green stems. Conditioning: cut the stems on the slant and give them a good drink of water.

### Senecio greyii
This is a useful evergreen or ever-grey shrub with thick grey leaves, margined silver-grey, white underneath. Flowers are daisy-like and deep yellow. Very attractive if used whilst flowers are in bud form. Conditioning: hammer ends and place in hot water.

### Skimmia
Evergreen shrub with clusters of white flowers, star-like, sweet-smelling and very attractive in spring with their leaves stripped off to expose the flowers. It also has .red berries in the winter which are good to use in place of non-existent holly berries. S. japonica 'Rubella' is very pretty with red buds

This group of flowers on a black marble pedestal was used as an entrance group for a wedding in July. It consisted of all white flowers with pale green foliage and silver leaves. The flowers were delphiniums, *Lilium auratum*, paeonies and gladioli. Foliage used was stripped lime, philadelphus, trails of variegated ivy and a plant of *Caladium* 'Candidum'.

and pinkish, scented flowers. Conditioning: hammer stems and put in warm water. Spray berries with leaf shine.

### *Stachys lanata* (Lamb's Tongue)
The leaves are grey-white and very useful for small arrangements; the flower spikes are borne on tall grey stems covered with pink/purple flowers. They are very useful for drying by hanging up. Conditioning: place stems in warm water and give them a long drink.

### *Symphoricarpos albus* (Snowberry)
Clusters of white berries on long stems; it is best to expose the berries by removing the leaves. 'Magic Berry' is a good pink variety of *S.* × *doorentosii*; the white *S. rivularis* keeps its berries on the bush most of the winter after the leaves have fallen. Conditioning: hammer stems and place in hot water.

### *Syringa* (Lilac)
A large family of free-flowering trees and bushes, bearing trusses of flowers in shades of purple, white, pink and yellow. Conditioning: remove all the leaves, hammer the stems, and place them in hot water with a handful of sugar.

### *Tellima grandiflora*
Pretty heart-shaped leaves, flowers are insignificant on tall stems – small green bells tinged with pink. The leaves are very useful all the year round. *T. purpurea* has deep purple leaves in winter. Conditioning: cut stems of leaves and flowers and place in boiling water.

### *Thalictrum* (Meadow Rue)
*T. flavum glaucum* has hardy tall stems of blue grey leaves with yellow fluffy flowers. The leaves are very useful in conjunction with sweet peas. Conditioning: cut stems and place in hot water.

### *Tilia* (Lime)
Quite one of the best trees for flower arrangers. Remove leaves to expose the flowers. Conditioning: hammer stems well and give them a long drink.

### *Tulipa* (Tulip)

A large genus very popular with flower arrangers who have a wealth of varieties to choose from. My favourites are the double white 'Mount Tacoma', cottage tulips, 'Apricot Beauty', the green *Tulipa viridiflora*, and 'Artist' streaked with apricot and green. The lily-flowered tulips are very stately in many lovely colours. But to me, the most attractive for mixed arrangements of spring flowers are the Rembrandt tulips loved by the Dutch flower painters. Conditioning: cut off the white end of the stem and wrap in newspaper, then put in warm water with sugar. Also you can prick the stem just under the bloom to stop drooping.

### *Ulmus glabra* (Wych Elm)

This valuable tree with its winged pale green seed heads in spring is very effective when used in a vase with mixed green foliage.

### *Viburnum*

Hardy flowering shrubs. The best known is *V. opulus* 'Sterile', the snowball tree. They are best used when the balls are in their green form. *V. fragrans* has pink flowers, sweetly scented, from December onwards. *V. tinus*, laurustinus, is a useful evergreen flowering pinky/white in the winter. Conditioning: hammer stems and place in hot water before arranging.

### *Weigela*

Very useful shrub with pink flowers appearing in midsummer when there is little else in flowering shrubs available. There is one with variegated foliage which is called *W. florida* 'Variegata' and is very beautiful. Conditioning: hammer stems and place in hot water.

### *Zinnia*

This is a useful and colourful daisy type flower, ranging in colours from red to green taking in the dusky pinks, creams and mauves. Conditioning: cut stems and place in 2·5cm/1in hot water. To strengthen stem push a thick florist's wire through the head into the stem.